MONEY, ACCUMULATION
AND CRISIS

LONDON AND NEW YORK

FUNDAMENTALS OF PURE AND APPLIED ECONOMICS

EDITORS IN CHIEF

J. LESOURNE, Conservatoire National des Arts et Métiers, Paris, France
H. SONNENSCHEIN, University of Pennsylvania, Philadelphia, PA, USA

ADVISORY BOARD

K. ARROW, Stanford, CA, USA
W. BAUMOL, Princeton, NJ, USA
W. A. LEWIS, Princeton, NJ, USA
S. TSURU, Tokyo, Japan

MARXIAN ECONOMICS I
In 3 Volumes

MONEY, ACCUMULATION AND CRISIS

DUNCAN K FOLEY

LONDON AND NEW YORK

First published in 1986 by
Harwood Academic Publishers GmbH

Reprinted in 2001 by
Routledge
2 Park Square, Milton Park, Abingdon, Oxon, OX14 4RN

Simultaneously published in the USA and Canada by Routledge

711 Third Avenue, New York, NY 10017

Transferred to Digital Printing 2007

Routledge is an imprint of the Taylor & Francis Group, an informa business

First issued in paperback 2013

British Library Cataloguing in Publication Data
A CIP catalogue record for this book
is available from the British Library

Money, Accumulation and Crisis
ISBN 978-0-415-26984-1 (hbk)
ISBN 978-0-415-86613-2 (pbk)

Money, Accumulation and Crisis

Duncan K Foley

Barnard College of Columbia University, USA

A Volume in the Marxian Economics Section
edited by
John E Roemer
University of California, Davis, USA

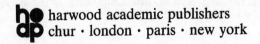 harwood academic publishers
chur · london · paris · new york

© 1986 by Harwood Academic Publishers GmbH, Poststrasse 22, 7000 Chur, Switzerland. All rights reserved.

Harwood Academic Publishers

P.O. Box 197
London WC2E 9PX
England

58, rue Lhomond
75005 Paris
France

P.O. Box 786
Cooper Station
New York, New York 10276
United States of America

Library of Congress Cataloging in Publication Data
Foley, Duncan K.
   Money, accumulation, and crisis.
   (Fundamentals of pure and applied economics,
ISSN 0883-2366; vol. 2. Marxian economics section)
   Bibliography: p.
   Includes index.
   1. Capitalism.   2. Marxian economics.   3. Social conflict.   I. Title.   II. Series:
Fundamentals of pure and applied economics; v. 2.   III.   Series: Fundamentals of pure
applied economics. Marxian economics section.
HB501.F64   1986   330.12'2   86-3144
ISBN 3-7186-0280-6

CONTENTS

INTRODUCTION TO THE SERIES

Drawing on a personal network, an economist can still relatively easily stay well informed in the narrow field in which he works, but to keep up with the development of economics as a whole is a much more formidable challenge. Economists are confronted with difficulties associated with the rapid development of their discipline. There is a risk of "balkanisation" in economics, which may not be favourable to its development.

Fundamentals of Pure and Applied Economics has been created to meet this problem. The discipline of economics has been subdivided into sections (listed on the inside back cover). These sections include short books, each surveying the state of the art in a given area.

Each book starts with the basic elements and goes as far as the most advanced results. Each should be useful to professors needing material for lectures, to graduate students looking for a global view of a particular subject, to professional economists wishing to keep up with the development of their science, and to researchers seeking convenient information on questions that incidentally appear in their work.

Each book is thus a presentation of the state of the art in a particular field rather than a step by step analysis of the development of the literature. Each is a high level presentation but accessible to anyone with a solid background in economics, whether engaged in business, government, international organizations, teaching, or research in related fields.

Three aspects of *Fundamentals of Pure and Applied Economics* should be emphasized:

—First, the project covers the whole field of economics, not only theoretical or mathematical economics.

—Second, the project is open-ended and the number of books is not predetermined. If new interesting areas appear, they will generate additional books.

—Last, all the books making up each section will later be grouped to constitute one or several volumes of an Encyclopaedia of Economics.

The editors of the sections are outstanding economists who have selected as authors for the series some of the finest specialists in the world.

J Lesourne   H Sonnenschein

Money, accumulation, and crisis

DUNCAN K. FOLEY

1. INTRODUCTION

THIS ESSAY presents the outlines of a theory of macroeconomics
based on Marx's theory of capitalist production and accumulation. The central unifying concept is the *circuit of capital*, which
views the circular flow of commodities and money from the
perspective of the income statements and balance sheets of
capitalist firms. Capitals motivated by the pursuit of profits to
accumulate, rather than households motivated by utility maxi-
mation through consumption, are the basic economic agents in
this framework. Household and state economic behavior are
included in the framework, but play a subsidiary role.

The essay begins by reconsidering the labor theory of value,
explaining the relations in Marx's theory between commodities
and money and between money prices and labor time. The key
simplifying idea in this discussion is the notion that the aggregate
value added in money terms produced by a system of capital is an
expression of the aggregate labor time newly expended in production. The ratio of the labor time to money value added I call the
value of money. This approach interprets the claims of the labor
theory of value as applying exactly in the aggregate, but not
necessarily to the prices of particular commodities, thus eliminat-
ing major problems in the traditional treatment of the relation
between value and price. In this interpretation the labor theory of
value becomes a natural and powerful foundation for macroeconomic theory, which is concerned precisely with these aggregate flows of value.

The essay continues by reviewing Marx's theory of capitalist
production and of surplus value. The central idea here is that the
emergence of labor-power as a commodity sold on the market for

a wage creates a fundamental division of aggregate value added between wages and surplus value, and a parallel division of social labor time between paid and unpaid labor.

The ability of capital to appropriate surplus value is the foundation of the circuit of capital. Value moves continually from the form of money into means of production and labor-power, then into newly produced commodities containing surplus value, and back into money again through sale, thus preparing the next round of the circuit. The circular motion of the aggregate social capital is the object of analysis of a Marxist macroeconomic theory.

The development of a mathematical representation of the circuit of capital allows us to resolve questions of steady-state growth (which Marx calls *expanded reproduction*) and to pose the problem of the instability of capital accumulation. I make explicit within this framework the Keynesian notion that sources of money demand must be sought within the circuit of capital itself, in the capital outlays of capitalist firms. This analysis shows the close connection between the expansion of credit and the continued expansion of the circuit of capital. This link is studied both by comparing steady-state paths, and by examining arbitrary paths of the model. These results are extended to situations where the value of money varies over time in response to changes in the average tightness of the market for produced commodities.

In order to make the comparison of this labor theory of value based macroeconomics with Keynesian and neoclassical macroeconomic theory clearer, theories of credit, interest, and central bank policy that are consistent with circuit of capital macroeconomics are outlined.

The most intriguing aspect of the circuit of capital approach is the possibility of systematically modelling non-linearities in the system that could give rise to instabilities and crises in the accumulation of capital. The problems of proportionality between different Departments of production, of changes in the basic parameters of profitability with accumulation, and the specific nature of crises of capital accumulation are the subjects of the last sections.

The macroeconomic theory that emerges from this study has some technical features that are of interest.

In the circuit of capital model the availability of non-produced resources, including labor-power, enters only through the impact shortages or surpluses have on the parameters of profitability that govern the model. The proximate limit to capitalist production is the availability of capital, that is, accumulated surplus value. This point of view allows us to analyze the dynamics of capital coherently without the notion of full employment of labor, and without the confusions raised by the concepts of voluntary and involuntary unemployment. The circuit of capital models offer a more direct theory of the volume of employment itself.

The circuit of capital framework offers a unified and powerful method for dealing with the problems of stocks and flows (see Ref. 46 for a discussion of the difficulties in traditional treatments of these issues). The basic elements of analysis are flows of value and time lags in the various phases of the circuit. These time lags give rise to stocks of value in various forms as a consequence of the pattern of flows. This treatment can be applied uniformly to all stocks of value, to financial assets as well as to productive assets.

Finally, the circuit of capital theory replaces the concept of equilibrium, which has muddied macroeconomic thinking, with the more natural concept of determinate paths for the value flows in the capitalist economy. The system of capitals is seen as being in continuous but determinate motion, not as heading for some (possibly shifting) equilibrium state. It is possible to define properties of paths that have equilibrium-like characteristics, such as stationarity or stability of stock-flow ratios, but the analysis is not bound to such constructions.

In writing this essay I have tried to synthesize disparate strands of economic thought. The references in general indicate the broad sources which contribute to this synthesis rather than specific technical contributions. My aim is to chart a theory in which the main ideas of macroeconomics from different schools can find their proper places.

2. PRICE AND VALUE[1]

Because so much misunderstanding has collected around the idea of value, it may help to begin with the most elementary considerations.

In ordinary language a commodity has a price, the amount of something else (usually money) for which it can be exchanged. A collection of commodities whose prices are expressed in the same units have a value, the sum of the product of each commodity's price and the quantity of it in the collection. If v is value, p_j the price of commodity j, and q_j the quantity of commodity j,

$$v = p_1 q_1 + \ldots + p_n q_n. \qquad (2.1)$$

There are two different ways of interpreting this relation. Modern economic theory tends to view prices and quantities as the fundamental objects of scientific explanation, and value merely as a way of summing up the prices of commodities.[2]

The classical economists and Marx, on the other hand, viewed value itself as a fundamental object of investigation, with its own laws and determinants that were prior to the determination of price. With this starting point prices appear as a device for *distributing* value over the commodities on the right-hand-side of equation (2.1). There is nothing "metaphysical" in this view as long as the theory specifies clearly what social laws the value concept is supposed to express.

In what follows particular interest attaches to the value newly produced in an economy in a period of time, the aggregate *value added*, or the value of the net product once the value of means of production used up has been deducted. If the economy is a national economy, this is the familiar Net National Product of national income accounting.

Very little can be said about the concept of value without introducing further theoretical ideas. If the concept of value is to have any meaning, however, it must exhibit some invariance

---

1.   The argument of this section was developed in conversation with G. Dumenil.
2.   Thus Debreu [3] explains value by investigating the determinants of price in a static market clearing framework.

properties. At a minimum, a uniform proportional change in all prices should leave the value unchanged (or equivalently, should alter the units in which we measure value in the inverse proportion). What other changes in prices and quantities leave value invariant is the subject of theories of value.

The value approach to economic theory essentially argues that we can distinguish between explanatory laws that govern the total value produced and those that determine the distribution of this value through prices to the commodities produced. This point of view may be contrasted with the notion that only prices are determinate, that is, that the only laws are those governing price.

3. COMMODITY, VALUE, AND MONEY

In a commodity producing society, products are the property of particular economic agents and are exchanged through bargaining. The commodity thus has two aspects: its usefulness, or, in Smith's language, use value, which makes it an object of interest to someone in the society, and is a necessary condition for it to exchange for other commodities; and its power to exchange for other commodities. The system of exchange establishes exchange ratios between all the commodities in the system: 1 bushel of wheat = 10 pounds of oranges, and so on.

The point of view of the theory of value hypothesizes that these exchange ratios express a common social substance, *value*, contained in or carried by the commodities. It is possible to see any collection of commodities as carrying a certain amount of value, which is distributed among the commodities in proportion to the exchange ratios. The exchange ratios express only the *relative* amounts of value assigned to the various commodities. In order to express the absolute amount of value it is necessary to construct some measure of value.

The values of all the commodities can be expressed in terms of a *general equivalent* (which may be a particular commodity, or an abstract standard). Marx proposes that money is a *socially accepted general equivalent*, a general equivalent commonly used in a commodity producing society to express the value of the commodities.

Money is thus an expression of value separate from particular commodities, or a form of value.

This proposal insists that money is inherent in the commodity form of production itself. This suggests that an attempt to develop a theory of commodity exchange without money (a "barter economy") and then to introduce money (as, for example, a device to minimize transaction costs (see Ref. 35, 37, and 40 for examples) involves a fallacy, since important functions of money are already posited in the barter economy (cf Ref. 2 for an account of models in which all commodities are implicitly assumed to be money).

This point of view also requires us to distinguish between the problem of the money form of value (how value can appear separately from particular commodities), and the problem of forms of money (what social devices, for example, the emergence of a money commodity, or of credit denominated in abstract monetary units, perform monetary functions in particular societies).

4. VALUE AND LABOR

Classical economic theory, reaching its high point in Ricardo, goes further and identifies the value in collections of commodities with the human labor expanded in their production. This idea arises from the global, social point of view of classical theory, which sees property rights and the commodity form of production as devices to organize and allocate human productive activity (labor). This idea makes no sense from a local or particular perspective, since there are many ways to secure value in a commodity producing society besides expending labor in production. The labor theory of value is the assertion that different explanatory principles govern the production of value at a social level (the expenditure of labor) and its distribution among various agents though prices.

The labour theory of value leads to many paradoxes unless the level of abstraction at which it holds is specified precisely. Marx undertook to clarify and refine Ricardo's formulation of the labor theory of value to eliminate these paradoxes. The important results of his critique are the following (see Ref. 44 for a full account of these critical results):

1. Although the forms of value, money and price appear pervasively throughout commodity producing societies, the origin of value is in the new production of commodities through the expenditure of labor. It is necessary to develop the principles governing the production of value before treating problems of the exchange of old or non-produced things (land, rare paintings, and so forth).

2. In considering the new production of value, the principle that value arises from the expenditure of labor applies at the level of the aggregate of newly produced commodities. Thus the aggregate value added in money terms in commodity production in a period is an expression of the total social labor expended in that period. The ratio of total productive social labor time to aggregate value added is called the *value of money* (or the *monetary expression of value*, see Ref. 1, 5, 7, 11, 25) and is denominated in hours of social labor per unit of money.

3. The fact that labor is expended in commodity production means that in addition to its concrete properties (as weaving, building, or information processing labor) labor has a general *abstract* property, its power to produce value.

4. Labor expended outside the system of commodity production produces no value in this sense (although it may in a larger social sense be necessary labor: see Ref. 10, 16, 21, 50). This is to say that *social* labor produces value.

5. The equalization of commodity prices in exchange implies that labor expended in the current socially most efficient methods of production governs the value of commodities. Thus labor expended in excess of what is socially necessary does not produce value.

We may sum up these points by saying that the aggregate money value added in a commodity producing society is an expression of the aggregate abstract, social, necessary labor expended in producing the net commodity product. In what follows I will assume that the reader recalls these important qualifications, and will write 'labor' for 'abstract, social, necessary labor'.

The labor theory of value in Marx's interpretation argues that the principles governing the production of new value lie in the amount and mode of utilization of social labor in a commodity producing society.

This value may be redistributed in the exchange of the commodities produced. The price of a particular commodity less the costs of non-labor inputs to its production (its value added) may, given the monetary expression of value, be the equivalent of more or less labor time than was actually bestowed on the commodity in its production. This gives rise to *unequal exchange*, in which a commodity has a price that is the equivalent of more or less labor time than is actually contained in it. Unequal exchange arises from differences in the bargaining positions of commodity owners and especially the degree of competition on both sides of the market for a commodity. In the aggregate, value added is proportional to the total labor expended.

Claims to part of the newly produced value may be exchanged against property rights in old or non-produced things. For example, the ownership of land, the right to exclude other agents from it, because it allows the owner to collect a rent from the stream of newly produced value, will exchange for a claim to part of that newly produced value. Land has a price, though it has no value.

5. CAPITALIST PRODUCTION

Marx conceives of *capital* as self-expanding value. In contrast with the behavior of agents who exchange commodities through the medium of money to achieve a more satisfactory consumption of use-values, a capital buys and sells commodities for the sake of the increment in value it can appropriate in that process. Capital begins with money (in some form or other, including financially denominated claims), which it uses to buy means of production and labor power. The expenditure of labor in production transforms the means of production into a new qualitatively different use-value, a finished commodity that carries the value of those means of production and the value added by the labor expended. This finished commodity is then sold for money, returning the costs of means of production and labor power together with an incremental value, or *surplus value*. The surplus value together with the wages paid to purchase labor power comprise the value added. The money value added in this sense corresponds in the aggregate to the total social labor expended in the production of commodities, although any particular commodity may have a price that deviates from the direct and indirect labor expended in the production of that commodity.

The labor theory of value implies that the value added in the aggregate is an expression of expended social labor. Workers receive only a part of this value added in the form of wages. The wage is the price of labor power. If we multiply the wage by the monetary expression of value, we express the wage in terms of hours of abstract labor received by workers per hour of labor power sold, which Marx calls the *value of labor-power*. (Here I assume that one hour of labor-power sold corresponds to one hour of labor expended. The value of labor-power is normalized to an hour of labor-power.) The proximate source of surplus value is the fact that the value of labor-power is less than unity, so that productive workers as a class receive an equivalent in wages for only a fraction of the labor time they actually expend. The ratio of surplus value to wages, which is an alternative method of describing the division of social labor time between wages and surplus value, Marx calls the *rate of exploitation* or the *rate of surplus value*.

The labor theory of value also requires us to distinguish between wages and the costs of other means of production. The value of other means of production than labor power reappears unchanged in the total value of output, and is thus, from the point of view of the labor theory of value, a non-expanding or *constant capital*. The value of wages reappears in the value of output sold augmented by the addition of the surplus value and is thus expanding or *variable capital*. One of the main explanatory claims of the labor theory of value is that changes in constant capital and variable capital have different effects on the amount of surplus value produced.

The aggregate surplus value is paid out in a variety of forms: as the wages and salaries of administrative and sales employees; as fees for legal and financial business services; as interest payments on borrowed money capital; as direct and indirect taxes; and finally as the profit of the capital itself.

The level of the value of labor-power is obviously a variable of critical importance to a capitalist economic system. The general level of the value of labor-power must reflect the relation between the standard of living of workers and average labor productivity in the system. Capitalist economic systems normally function with a margin of potentially employable workers, which Marx calls the *reserve army of labor*. In Marx's view the exhaustion of this reserve, if it occurs, will be automatically offset by the contraction in surplus value and hence capital accumulation and demand for labor-power that results from a rise in the value of labor-power. Here is a main point of contrast with neoclassical general equilibrium theory, which assumes full utilization of all resources, including labor, and sees the limiting factor in the rise of the value of labor-power with full employment as the psychological reluctance of capitalists to accumulate rather than consume as the rate of profit falls.

Capital is self-expanding value, but the secret of its expansion is the exploitation of labor through the mechanism of the wage.

6. THE CIRCUIT OF CAPITAL

The flow of value through a capitalist enterprise, or group of enterprises, can be thought of as a circuit. In qualitative terms this circuit shows the sequence of forms value takes in capitalist production:

$$M - C\{(MP, LP) \dots (P) \dots C' - M'\} = M + \Delta M \qquad (6.1)$$

where value in the form of money (M) is used to purchase commodities (C), namely means of production and labor-power (MP, LP) which pass through the production process (P) to become a new commodity (C') which in turn is sold for money (M') which comprises the return of the original money capital, M, and a surplus value (ΔM).

This motion of value is also summarized in the income or profit-and-loss statement of capitalist accounting practice:

Sales	$M' = M + \Delta M$
less labor costs	LP
less nonlabor costs	MP
(including depreciation)	
equals gross profit on sales	ΔM
or surplus value	(6.2)

The aim of the circuit of capital is the expansion of value, in contrast with the circuit of commodity exchange

$$C - M - C' \qquad (6.3)$$

where commodities of a given value are sold for money to purchase a different bundle of commodities of the same value. In particular the $C - M - C'$ circuit comes to an end with the purchase of the final bundle C', since the economic agent has transformed its value into the most desirable attainable collection of use-values. The $C - M - C'$ circuit can be renewed only by an external recreation of its initial conditions, where the economic agent possesses a group of commodities that is not its most desired collection among all those of the same value. The $M - C \ldots (P) \ldots C' - M'$ circuit, on the other hand, recreates its own initial conditions, namely a mass of money value in tension with its own possibility of expansion through the circuit of capital.[3]

The fundamental object of study of Marxist economic theory is an ensemble of capitals traversing the circuit of capital. The problem is to understand the characteristic behavior of such a system driven proximately by the pursuit of surplus value. Each capital may, of course, have many value flows in different phases of the circuit at any one moment.

---

3. Neoclassical economic theory, since it acknowledges only the pursuit of use-value as an ultimately rational end of human activity, cannot conceptualize capital accumulation as a self-determined phenomenon, and in its place studies economic growth driven by changes in external variables like population or resource availability. Patinkin [40] exemplifies the dilemmas of the C–M–C' approach in his parable of "manna".

Each phase of the circuit of capital takes some time for its completion. A certain period elapses between the hiring of labor-power and the purchase of means of production to begin the process and the emergence of a finished commodity at its end. Likewise, a finished commodity waits for a certain length of time before it is sold for money, and the money proceeds from sales stay in the hands of the firm for a period in the form of money before being spent to purchase labor-power and means of production to start a new phase of the circuit. Thus at any moment in time we would find certain stocks of value in each of the phases of the circuit of capital. The asset side of the balance sheet of a capitalist firm measures these stocks:

Assets

Financial assets	} Money capital
Inventories of raw materials and partly finished goods	
Undepreciated long-lived assets	} Productive capital
Inventories of finished goods awaiting sale	} Commercial capital (6.4)

The size of these stocks of value depend on the historical flows of value through the circuit and on the structure of time lags in production. In this conception the flows of value are fundamental, the stocks arising as an incidental consequence of the fact that it takes some time for value to traverse each phase of the circuit of capital.

A convenient way of modelling the circuit of capital mathematically is to use convolutions to link flows of value in different parts of the circuit. For example, we can regard a dollar laid out to purchase labor-power and means of production at a certain time t as emerging in the form of finished commodities at later times, perhaps distributed over a whole interval of the future. The pattern of output may be a simple time delay of duration T in production. A dollar of capital outlay at time 0 waits for the period T and then emerges all at once in the form of a finished commodity. On the other hand, more general cases exist in which the value of the capital outlay at time 0 emerges gradually and continuously over the future. The integral of the distribution describing this time pattern over the whole positive half line must be equal to 1, since all the value laid out as capital must emerge sooner or later from production. This method can describe quite general temporal patterns of input-output relations. For example, some of the capital outlay may experience a simple time delay (circulating capital) and some may emerge uniformly in the value of finished products over a period (uniformly depreciating fixed capital) (cf Ref. 54).

To construct a model of the circuit of aggregate social capital, let $C(t)$ be the flow of value of capital outlays at time t: $P(t)$ the flow of value of finished commodities emerging from production at time t, including surplus value; $R(t)$ the flow of value of realization, including surplus value at time t; $a(., t')$ the time profile of production lags for capital laid out at time t'; $b(., t')$ the time profile of realization lags for finished commodities emerging at time t'; $c(., t')$ the time profile of lags in the recommital of money realized at time t' to production; $q(t')$ the value markup (the ratio of surplus value to costs of production) on capital laid out at time t'; and $p(t')$ the proportion of surplus value realized at time t' that is recommited to production.

According to the labor theory of value, in the aggregate value is created only by the expenditure of social labor. If the money wage at time t' is $w(t')$, the monetary expression of value $m(t')$ (the ratio that expresses the labor time equivalent to an hour's labor), and the fraction of capital outlays going to the purchase of labor-power at time t' is $k(t')$, the total labor hours set in motion at time t' are $(k(t')C(t'))/w(t')$. This labor time has the money equivalent at time $t'(k(t')C(t')/w(t')m(t')$, since $1/m(t')$ is the monetary expression of the value added by an hour of labor at time t'. The surplus value arising from this labor time is just $(1 - w(t')m(t'))(k(t')C(t')/w(t')m(t'))$, and the markup $q(t')$ is

$$q(t') = \frac{(1 - w)mk}{wm} = ek \qquad (6.5)$$

where $e(t')$ is the rate of surplus value at time t'. The money surplus value realized by capital may be larger or smaller than this if the monetary expression of value changes between the time capital is laid out and time of realization of the finished commodity. For the moment assume that the value of money is constant through time.

The parameter p is necessary because not all of the surplus value realized is recommitted to production. Some part is spent on the consumption of capitalists, is taxed and spend by the State, or is used up in unproductive expenditures of capitalist firms.

Given these basic parameters, the flows in the circuit of capital are related by the convolutions:

$$P(t) = \int_{-\infty}^{t} C(t')\,(1 + q(t'))a(t - t';\ t')\ dt' \quad (6.6a)$$

$$Q(t) = \int_{-\infty}^{t} C(t')a(t - t';\ t')\ dt' \quad (6.6b)$$

$$R(t) = \int_{-\infty}^{t} P(t')b(t - t';\ t')\ dt' \quad (6.7a)$$

$$R'(t) = \int_{-\infty}^{t} Q(t')b(t - t';\ t')\ dt' \quad (6.7b)$$

$$R''(t) = \int_{-\infty}^{t} (P(t') - Q(t')b(t - t';\ t')\ dt' \quad (6.7c)$$

$$C(t) = \int_{-\infty}^{t} (R'(t') + p(t')R''(t'))c(t - t';\ t')\ dt'$$

$$(6.8)$$

Here $R'(t')$ is the part of realization that corresponds to the recovery of capital outlays, and $R''(t')$ is the part that corresponds to the realization of surplus value. $Q(t')$ is the flow of the value of finished commodities at cost.

If $F(t)$ is aggregate financial capital, $N(t)$ aggregate productive capital, and $X(t)$ aggregate commodity capital, we have the relations:

$$dF(t)/dt = R'(t) + p(t)R''(t) - C(t) \quad (6.9)$$

$$dN(t)/dt = C(t) - Q(t) \quad (6.10)$$

$$dX(t)/dt = P(t) - S(t) \quad (6.11)$$

The relations (6.6)–(6.11) describe the flow of value through the aggregate social circuit of capital in a completely general fashion, since the time lag profiles may vary arbitrarily over time.

7. SIMPLE AND EXPANDED REPRODUCTION

In a real capitalist economy the reinvestment of surplus value in production constantly expands the aggregate social capital, which is the phenomenon of *accumulation*. Real accumulation involves the constant revolutionizing of the production process: the adoption of new techniques of production, often on a larger scale, the creation of new products, the reorganization of capitals, and so on. These qualitative changes in production find their reflection in changes in the parameters that govern the circuit of capital, the composition of capital outlays (*k* in the notation of the last section), the value of labor-power (*wm*, or *e*) which determine the value markup (*q*), the rate of capitalization (*p*), and the production, realization and finance lags.

As a first step toward analyzing these complex, and necessarily nonlinear problems, let us consider the imaginary situation of a capitalist economy that reproduces itself without changes in the underlying parameters. This is the exercise Marx, Ref. 28, II, ch XX, XXI, calls the analysis of the *simple* and *expanded* reproduction of capital. Marx's analysis there focusses on the problem of proportionality between production of means of production and means of subsistence. To begin with I will abstract from this problem and look at the aggregate value conditions for reproduction.

Analytically the assumption of simple and expanded reproduction requires that the parameters *p*, *q*, and the lag functions *a*(.), *b*(.) and *c*(.) of the model set out above be constant through time. When this is true the basic equations become:

$$P(t) = (1 + q) \int_{-\infty}^{t} C(t')a(t - t') \, dt' \qquad (7.1a)$$

$$Q(t) = \int_{-\infty}^{t} C(t')a(t - t') \, dt \qquad (7.1b)$$

$$R(t) = \int_{-\infty}^{t} P(t')b(t-t')\,dt \tag{7.2a}$$

$$R'(t) = \int_{-\infty}^{t} Q(t')b(t-t')\,dt' \tag{7.2b}$$

$$R''(t) = \int_{-\infty}^{t} (P(t')-Q(t'))b(t-t')\,dt \tag{7.2c}$$

$$C(t) = \int_{-\infty}^{t} (R'(t')+pR''(t'))c(t-t')\,dt' \tag{7.3}$$

Simple or expanded reproduction correspond to exponential growth paths for all the flows of value. Since the system is homogeneous of first degree in the absolute size of the flow $C(t)$, normalize by assuming $C(0) = 1$, so that $C(t) = \exp(gt)$ for an unknown growth rate g on an exponential path. By successive substitution we reach:

$$P(0) = (1+q)a^*(g) \tag{7.4a}$$
$$Q(0) = a^*(g) \tag{7.4b}$$
$$R(0)\ (1+q)a^*(g)b^*(g) \tag{7.5a}$$
$$R'(0) = a^*(g)b^*(g) \tag{7.5b}$$
$$R''(0) = qa^*(g)b^*(g) \tag{7.5c}$$
$$C(0) = 1 = (1+pq)a^*(g)b^*(g)c^*(g) \tag{7.6}$$

where

$$a^*(s) = \int_0^{\infty} \exp(-st')a(t')\,dt' \tag{7.7}$$

which is the Laplace transform of the transfer function $a(.)$, and similarly for $b^*(s)$ and $c^*(s)$. Since the lag functions are nonnegative and integrate to 1 over the positive half-line, we have (assuming that the lags are not instantaneous):

$$a^*(0) = b^*(0) = c^*(0) = 1 \tag{7.8a}$$
$$da^*(s)/ds,\ db^*(s)/ds,\ dc^*(s)/ds < 0 \tag{7.8b}$$
$$\lim_{s\to} a^*(s) = \lim_{s\to} b^*(s) = \lim_{s\to} c^*(s) = 0 \tag{7.8c}$$

Equation (7.6) is the characteristic equation of the system. It has a unique positive real root g, the *expanded reproduction mode* of the system. When $g = 0$ the right hand side of (7.6) is $(1 + pq) > 1$ unless $pq = 0$. If $pq = 0$ the rate of growth is zero, corresponding to what Marx calls *simple reproduction*. If $pq > 0$, the right hand side of (7.6) is greater than 1 for $g = 0$, but declines monotonically to zero as g increases. Thus there will be a unique positive g for which (7.6) is satisfied.

Solution of (6.9)–(6.11) yields the aggregate balance sheet ratios of the system:

$$F(0) = (1 + pq)a^*(g)b^*(g)(1 - c^*(g))/g \qquad (7.9)$$

$$N(0) = (1 - a^*(g))/g \qquad (7.10)$$

$$X(0) = a^*(g)(1 - b^*(g))/g \qquad (7.11)$$

These are all positive at the growth rate g and show the ratio of the assets to the current flow of capital outlays.

Conventional national income accounting focusses on the flows of value added, wages plus surplus value, in a national system of capitals. If $Y(t)$ is the value of net product including the markup, we have:

$$Y(t) = P(t) - \int_{-\infty}^{t} (1 - k(t'))C(t')a(t - t'; t') \, dt' \qquad (7.12)$$

In the case of simple or expanded reproduction this simplifies to:

$$Y(0) = P(0) - (1 - k)Q(0) = (k + q)a^*(g) \qquad (7.13)$$

The dependence of the growth rate on the parameters of the system is easy to see from (7.6). A rise in pq raises the growth rate; any shift of $a(.)$ that lowers $a^*(s)$ for all s will also raise g, and similarly for $b(.)$ and $c(.)$.

The *rate of profit*, r, is the ratio of the realized surplus value to the total capital tied up in the system. On an exponential path this is:

$$r = R''/(F + N + X) = g/p \qquad (7.14)$$

This is the "Cambridge equation" linking the growth rate of the system, the profit rate, and the rate of capitalization of surplus value. (These results have a close relation to the growth theory results in Ref. 6. 20 and 22. See also Ref. 42. The relation between the profit rate and the growth rate has been given an elegant exposition in Ref 38.)

8. AGGREGATE DEMAND IN THE CIRCUIT OF CAPITAL

The model of expanded reproduction developed in the last section abstracts from the problem of the source of aggregate money demand to realize produced commodities. It does this in assuming that the realization lag $b(.)$ is a given parameter of the system; sales are determined by production in this model.

In a closed capitalist economy (such as the world capitalist economy) the ultimate sources of aggregate demand are the capital outlays of firms to begin production, and realized surplus value. Capital outlays provide the demand for produced means of production and the wage incomes of worker households. Other household income arises from the wages of administrative, sales, and business services employees who do not produce new value, and from the dividends and interest paid to capitalist households (remembering that some households may have both labor and property income), both paid out of realized surplus value. State expenditure is ultimately financed by taxes on surplus value or incomes, or from the surplus value appropriated by State enterprises. There may be time lags in the spending of households or the State as well. The "life-cycle" and "permanent income" theories of household consumption can be expressed in terms of linear or nonlinear lags in consumption spending. See Ref. 23 and 14.

We can model aggregate demand in the circuit of capital by allowing the realization lag $b(.)$ to become a determined variable and specifying the dependence of aggregate demand on the flows of value in the circuit.

The sources of demand are:

$$D(t) = (1 - k(t))C(t) + \int_{-\infty}^{t} k(t')C(t')\, \mathrm{d}(t - t'; t')\, \mathrm{d}t'$$
$$+ \int_{-\infty}^{t} (1 - p(t'))R''(t')e(t - t'; t')\, \mathrm{d}t' + B'(t) \quad (8.1)$$

where the first term represents purchases of means of production, including gross investment in fixed capital, the second, workers' spending of wages (passed through the lag function $d(.)$), the third consumption and State spending out of surplus value (passed through the spending lag $e(.)$), and the last, $B'(t)$, household and State spending financed by new borrowing. The lags $d(.)$ and $e(.)$ have the same properties as we assumed for $a(.)$ in (7.8).

If $B'(t) = 0$, and capitals finance new production only out of past sales (as is implied by (6.8)), there will be insufficient aggregate demand on a path of expanded reproduction with a positive growth rate unless all the spending lags are zero. To see this, assume that $C(t) = \exp(gt)$, and that k, g, p, and the lag functions $a(.)$, $b(.)$, $c(.)$, $d(.)$, and $e(.)$ are all invariant through time. Then:

$$
\begin{aligned}
D(0) &= (1-k) + kd^*(g) + q(1-p)e^*(g)a^*(g)b^*(g) \\
&= (1 - k(1 - d^*(g)))(1 + pq)a^*(g)b^*(g)c^*(g) \\
&\quad + q(1-p)e^*(g)a^*(g)b^*(g) \\
&= a^*(g)b^*((g)[(1 - k(1 - d^*(g)))c^*(g) \\
&\quad + q(p(1 - k(1 - d^*(g)))c^*(g) + (1-p)e^*(g))] \\
&< a^*(g)b^*(g)(1 + q) = R(0) \qquad (8.2)
\end{aligned}
$$

since $d^*(g)$, $c^*(g)$, and $e^*(g) < 1$ for $g > 0$. On a path of expanded reproduction with no borrowing past sales are insufficient to realize current production because of lags in spending.

This problem has two practical solutions (see Ref. 26, 27, 28, II, ch XXI, and 13). First, in an economy where money is a produced commodity, like gold, the money commodity need not be sold in order to be realized as money value, since it is already in the money form of value. Thus the gap between aggregate money demand and the realization of produced commodities can be filled by gold production at the appropriate scale. If $S(t)$ is the value of the flow of sales at time t, and $G(t)$ is the value of the flow of gold production at time t:

$$
R(t) = S(t) + G(t) = D(t) + G(t) \qquad (8.3)
$$

On a path of expanded reproduction without borrowing we have $S(0) = D(0)$, and:

$$G(0) = R(0) - S(0)$$
$$= k(1 - d^*(g)) + q[(1 - (p(1 - k(1 - d^*(g))) + (1 - p)e^*(g)] \quad (8.4)$$

Second, this gap can be filled by new borrowing, either by capitals to finance capital outlays, by households to finance consumption spending, or by the State to finance its expenditure. To allow for capital outlays financed by debt, we reformulate (6.8) as:

$$C(t) = \int_{-\infty}^{t} (R'(t) + p(t')R''(t))c(t - t'; t') \, dt' + B(t) \quad (8.5)$$

where $B(t)$ is new capitalist borrowing.

The steady-state growth rate in expanded reproduction now corresponds to the size of new borrowing, since we have from (8.3) and (8.1):

$$R(0) = D(0) + G(0)$$
$$= [(1 - k(1 - d^*(g))) + B'(0) + G(0)](1 + q)/$$
$$[1 + q(1 - (1 - p)e^*(g))] \quad (8.6)$$

$$C(0) = 1 = (R'(0) + pR''(0))c^*(g) + B(0) \text{ or} \quad (8.7a)$$

$$1 - B(0) = c^*(g)R(0)[(1 + pq)/(1 + q)] \text{ or} \quad (8.7b)$$

$$1 = B(0) + \frac{c^*(g)[(1 - k(1 - d^*(g))) + B'(0) + G(0)](1 + pg)}{1 + q(1 - (1 - p)e^*(g))} \quad (8.7c)$$

The higher is g, the smaller is the right hand side of (8.7c) for given values of $B(0)$, $B'(0)$, $G(0)$, p, q, and the spending lag functions $c(.)$, $d(.)$ and $e(.)$. This expression shows that new non-capitalist borrowing and gold production play the same role in linking realization and production in the circuit of capital. The larger are B or $(B' + G)$ the higher will be the realized rate of expansion g.

But there is a limit to how high this rate of expansion can

become, imposed by the time lag in production and the social limits to the appropriation of surplus value. A higher g is achieved by reducing the realization lag, and in that fashion accelerating the motion of value around the circuit. This reduction in realization time cannot proceed beyond the point where the realization lag is zero.

To study this limit mathematically, we need an explicit expression for the realization lag $b(.)$. The simplest way to make $b(.)$ endogenous is to assume that this lag is a simple time delay T, so that inventories of finished commodities awaiting sale are accounted for in the model on a first-in first-out basis. A commodity sold at time t has waited a period $T(t)$ to be sold. Given a path of production $Q(.)$ and a path of sales $S(.)$, the function $T(t)$ must satisfy the first-in first-out relation:

$$\int_{t-T(t)}^{t+\Delta t - T(t+\Delta t)} Q(t')\,dt' = \int_{t}^{t+\Delta t} S(t')\,dt' \tag{8.8}$$

The mean value theorem assures us that:

$$Q(t')[t - T(t+\Delta t) - T(t)] = S(t'')\Delta t \tag{8.9}$$

for t', t'' in the relevant intervals. Dividing by t and taking the limit as $t - > 0$, we get:

$$Q(t - T(t))[1 - dT/dt] = S(t) \text{ or} \tag{8.10a}$$

$$\frac{dT}{dt} = 1 - \frac{S(t)}{Q(t - T(t))} \tag{8.10b}$$

The speed of expansion of the system is limited by the requirement that T be nonnegative. On a steady-state path T is a constant, so we have from (8.10):

$$Q(t - T(t)) = S(t) \text{ or} \tag{8.11a}$$

$$Q(0)\exp(-gT) = S(0) \text{ or, from} \tag{8.11b}$$

$$T = (1/g)\ln(P(0)/S(0)) \geqslant 0, \tag{8.11c}$$

$$(1 + q(1 - (1-p)e^*(g)))a^*(g) \geqslant (1 - k(1 - d^*(g)))$$
$$+ B'(0) + (q/(1+q))e^*(g)(1-p)G(0) \tag{8.11d}$$

When $d^*(g) = e^*(g) = 1$ identically, and $G(0) = B'(0) = 0$, this simplifies to:

$$(1 + pq)a^*(g) \geqslant 1 \qquad (8.12)$$

The g^* for which $(1 + pq)a^*(g^*) = 1$ is a *limiting rate* of accumulation, given technology and the social relations of production.

A higher rate of gold production or of new borrowing raises the realized rate of expansion of this system by facilitating realization (which is, in effect, Keynes' discovery [23]) but this process ultimately runs into the barrier constituted by the most rapid growth rate compatible with the time lags in production and the rate of exploitation (the object of von Neumann's analysis [56]).

There is no immediate reason to think that a capitalist economy operating according to these principles will tend to create a demand for labor-power equal to the amount of labor-power the population can and will supply. In other words, there is no presumption that the capitalist system will reach a state of full employment, even when it is expanding at its maximal rate.

The rate for labor-power in the circuit of capital depends on the total capital circulating, the proportion, k, that is spent on labor-power and the wage, w. If L is the total demand for labor-power:

$$L(t) = kC(t)/w(t) \qquad (8.13)$$

A fall in money wages would increase the demand for labor-power instantaneously only if k were to fall by a smaller proportion. Since k reflects, in the short-run, primarily the technical proportions between labor and non-labor inputs to production required by the currently adopted techniques of production, it is likely that a fall in w will be matched by a fall in k, so that the demand for labor-power would not increase.

A fall in money wages, if the value of money remains stable, or rises by a smaller proportion, corresponds to a fall in the value of labor-power, and a rise in the rate of exploitation of productive labor. This change has two effects. By raising the rate of profit it may induce a switch in the techniques used to produce output, which would be reflected in a change in the technical proportions in which labor and nonlabor inputs enter production, as well as a revaluation of the nonlabor inputs themselves. This effect is studied in the literature on distribution, pricing, and choice of technique (see Ref. 15, 39 and 53). An important conclusion of this literature is that a rise in the rate of profit may not increase the demand for labor-power for a given flow of capital value.

The rise in the rate of profit that follows from a rise in the rate of exploitation has another, more certain, consequence for the demand for labor-power. An increase in the markup, q, resulting from a rise in the rate of exploitation, leads, if the capitalization rate does not fall in the same proportion, to a higher rate of accumulation of capital, and hence, for given k and w, to a more rapid growth of the demand for labor-power.

Thus the problem of the degree to which labor is employed in a capitalist system is complex and historical. It depends on the interaction of accumulation, technical change, and the movement of the value of labor-power, and on historical, sociological, and political factors that influence the potential labor-power available to the system. There is in this theory no presumption that accumulation and wage flexibility will lead to full employment of the potential available labor force, only a set of relations that can be used to investigate this question in a specific historical context.

Despite the possible irrelevance of a full-employment limit to capital accumulation, we have seen that there is another, internal limit to the accumulation of capital that arises from the inter-action of the rate of exploitation of labor and the time lags in production.

9. ACCUMULATION AND REALIZATION OUT OF THE STEADY STATE

The relations between new borrowing and the actual rate of growth of capitalist system derived in the last section were of a comparative dynamic type in that they compared fully realized steady-state paths of expanded reproduction.

These relations suggest that there is an intimate connection between aggregate demand and realized rates of increase in sales and production on arbitrary paths in the circuit of capital model. This connection brings us to the heart of classic Keynesian analyses, which emphasize the role of aggregate demand in governing the path of production in a capitalist economy.

The demand parameters on which Keynes focusses attention are propensities to consume, which govern household spending out of wage and nonwage income, and liquidity preference, which indirectly governs capitalist firms' spending on new investment. These parameters appear in the circuit of capital model as the spending lags $c(.)$, $d(.)$ and $e(.)$. The effect of aggregate demand on production in Keynesian models depends on the relation between sales and production, and the resulting movements of inventories of finished commodities awaiting sale. These effects are summed up in the circuit of capital model in the variable realization lag T. As T becomes larger capitals experience greater difficulty in selling their product, and a growth in inventories of finished commodities awaiting sale.

As Keynes argues in a static equilibrium framework, there is a close connection between the parameters governing aggregate demand and the state of realization in a capitalist economy.

To simplify the mathematical expressions involved, assume that the spending lags $c(.)$, $d(.)$ and $e(.)$ are all simple time delays with time constants T_f, T_w, and T_p respectively: a finance delay in capital spending, a wage delay in workers' household spending, and a profit delay in the spending of household revenues that arise from the flow of surplus value. The same first-in first-out reasoning as supported (8.10) leads, assuming no household or state borrowing, to the relations:

$$\frac{dT}{dt} = 1 - \frac{S(t)}{P(t - T)} \tag{9.1}$$

$$\frac{dT_w}{dt} = 1 - \frac{E_w(t)}{W(t - T_w)} = 1 - \frac{E_w(t)}{kC(t - T_w)} \tag{9.2}$$

$$\frac{dT_p}{dt} = 1 - \frac{E_p}{(1 - p)R''(t - T_p)} \tag{9.3}$$

$$\frac{dT_f}{dt} = 1 - \frac{C(t) - B(t)}{R'(t - T_f) + pR''(t - T_f)} \tag{9.4}$$

In this analysis, assume gold production is zero (or a monetary system not based on a commodity money), so that realization, R, is equal to sales, S. E_w is workers' household spending, W is wages, and E_p is household spending derived from revenues that are part of surplus value.

Suppose that an economy is on an arbitrary path consistent with the basic circuit of capital relations (6.6)–(6.8). We have, from (8.1) and (9.2)–(9.4):

$$S(t) = D(t) = E_w(t) + E_p(t) + (1 - k)C(t)$$

$$= [(1 - \mathrm{d}T_w/\mathrm{d}t)kC(t - T_w) + (1 - \mathrm{d}T_p/\mathrm{d}t)(1 - p)\,S''(t - T_p)$$

$$+ (1 - k)(1 - \mathrm{d}T_f/\mathrm{d}t)(S'(t - F_f) + pS''(t - T_f)) + (1 - k)B(t)$$

$$(9.5)$$

so that

$$\mathrm{d}T/\mathrm{d}t = 1 - [(1 - \mathrm{d}T_w/\mathrm{d}t)kC(t - T_w)$$

$$+ (1 - \mathrm{d}T_p/\mathrm{d}t)(1 - p)\,S''(t - T_p)$$

$$+ (1 - \mathrm{d}T_f/\mathrm{d}t)(1 - k)(S'(t - T_f) + pS''(t - T_f))$$

$$+ (1 - k)\,B(t)]/P(t - T) \qquad (9.6)$$

Thus on a path where spending lags are becoming longer (the derivatives of T_w, T_p, and T_f are negative) the realization lag T will also be rising faster than it would have if the spending delays were stable. Note also the important role that $B(t)$, capital outlays financed by new borrowing, plays in determining the path of the realization delay T.

Capital outlays financed by new borrowing create a flow of value to finance that new borrowing by realizing finished commodities held in inventory. If capitals borrow without spending the borrowed value on capital outlays, the finance time delay T_f will be increasing, by (9.4). If spending time delays are constant, an increase in capital outlays financed by new borrowing creates the flow of money value necessary to finance itself. This is a version of the Keynesian principle that the expansion of investment creates the saving necessary to finance itself.

The process of self-finance does, however, have a limit, namely the exhaustion of inventories of finished goods awaiting sale or (more broadly) of excess productive capacity. It is striking that this limit is internal to the circuit of capital, and need have no relation to the state of labor markets.

10. CHANGES IN THE VALUE OF MONEY

Upto this point I have abstracted from changes in the value of money, the ratio of aggregate labor time to aggregate value added.

In a commodity money system, one of the produced commodities, say, gold, becomes the socially accepted general equivalent. In this case the monetary unit (dollar, franc or whatever) is defined as being a certain amount of the money commodity (one U.S. dollar was originally 1/20th of an ounce of gold, for instance).

The gold price of a commodity in such a system tends to reflect the ratio between the price of production of that commodity (costs of inputs plus the average profit rate on the capital values tied up in production) and the price of production of gold. (Of course, further factors influencing the price of commodities, such as monopoly power or State intervention, may alter this relation.) In such a system the value of money tends to be equal to the aggregate labor time divided by the value added at the gold prices of commodities.

It sometimes happens that the State, especially under the fiscal pressures of war, issues paper "fiat" money that has no guaranteed rate of convertibility into gold. Leading examples are the British government's issue of paper pounds during the Napoleonic Wars, and the U.S. government's issue of greenback dollars during the Civil War. This paper money often goes to a discount against gold (a paper greenback dollar might be worth, say, only 50¢ in gold) because more paper is issued than could be absorbed by the circulation of currency in immediate transactions, or because of speculation on the military fortunes of the issuing State. In these cases the value of gold money continues to be determined by the price of production of gold relative to the price of production of other commodities. The existence of the fiat money merely raises the additional problem of the determinants of the discount between paper and gold.

In the twentieth century a new monetary situation evolved in which the relations between national monetary units (dollar, pound, franc, mark, etc.) and gold became weaker and weaker. This is different from the fiat money case, since now there is no gold money against which the dollar or pound or franc can be valued. In these circumstances the value of money is determined historically, by the inherited level of money prices assigned to commodities by producers on average, and by the average changes in those prices induced by the pricing strategies of capitals faced with a series of concrete conditions of demand. The value of money in this kind of system changes because on average the ensemble of capitalist firms raises or lowers the money prices of their products.

Such changes in the value of money may or may not lead to changes in the value of labor-power and the rate of exploitation, depending on the effectiveness with which workers defend the purchasing power of their wages.

Proximately, then, in such a system two important factors combine to determine the rate of change in the value of money. First, growth in average labor productivity tends to reduce the value of money, because less labor is expended per unit of use values produced. Second, average conditions of demand may permit capitals to raise the price per unit of use values, or may force them to lower prices per unit of use values. We can see these two factors if we write the value of money as the product of the price level and an index of average labor productivity:

$$
\begin{aligned}
m &= \frac{\text{aggregate labor time}}{\text{aggregate value added}} \\[2ex]
&= \frac{\text{labor time}}{\text{index of use values produced}} \\[2ex]
&\quad \times \frac{\text{index of use values produced}}{\text{value added}} \quad (10.1)
\end{aligned}
$$

Two problems arise in treating changes in the value of money within the circuit of capital framework. First, we need to distinguish between value flows measured in money terms and value flows measured in terms of social labor. Second, we need to propose some hypothesis as to what governs the historical evolution of the value of money.

The first problem is easily resolved conceptually. Adopt the convention that a variable prefixed with an asterisk is measured in money terms, and one without an asterisk is measured in terms of labor time. For example:

$$*C(t) = C(t)/m(t) \qquad (10.2)$$

We can write the aggregate demand as:

$$\begin{aligned}
*D(t) = {}& (1 - k(t))*C(t) \\
& + \int_{-\infty}^{t} k(t')*C(t')\, \mathrm{d}(t - t';\, t')\, \mathrm{d}t' \\
& + \int_{-\infty}^{t} (1 - p(t'))*R''(t')e(t - t';\, t')\, \mathrm{d}t' \\
& + *B'(t)
\end{aligned} \qquad (10.3)$$

This formulation implicitly assumes that the time profile of household spending streams depend on the time profile of money incomes. In other words, as the value of money changes households accept the labor value loss or gain on the principal value of their stocks of financial assets, and continue to spend the remainder in the same time pattern. An alternative conception would treat the changes in the value of money as current income, which would enter the households' spending lag process at the time it occurred.

We have, by a similar argument for firms:

$$*C(t) = \int_{-\infty}^{t} (*R'(t') + p(t')*R''(t'))c(t - t';\, t')\, \mathrm{d}t + *B(t) \qquad (10.4)$$

The aggregate demand dynamics now are modelled in money terms. We can translate these money flows, given a path of m, back into labor value flows by multiplying by the value of money.

$$C(t) = *C(t)m(t) \qquad (10.5)$$

$$R(t) = *R(t)m(t) \qquad (10.6)$$

What determines the path of the value of money? In a non-commodity-money system, the change in the value of money over a period depends on the average price change for commodities and the change in labor productivity over the same period. Suppose for the moment that we abstract from changes in labor productivity. It seems likely that the average change in money prices of commodities will depend on the average difficulty capitals have in selling commodities, which is conveniently measured by the time delay in selling commodities, T. A large T will signal difficulties in selling, so that capitals will not raise prices rapidly, and may be forced to lower them, and the value of money will be stable or rising. A small T signals ease in selling, conditions of strong demand on markets, rising prices, and a falling value of money.

$$\mathrm{d}m(t)/\mathrm{d}t = u(T), \text{ with } u' > 0 \qquad (10.7)$$

Notice that this formulation has no necessary connection with the state of the labor market. Changes in the value of money are a reflection of the underlying limits to the rate of accumulation imposed by the value of labor-power, the composition of capital, the capitalization rate, and the time lags of the system expressed by (8.11).

In the case of expanded reproduction we can easily see explicitly the relation between the value and money accounting categories. Suppose that $*R'(t)$ is the recovery of historic money costs in realization at time t, and $*R''(t)$ the realization of surplus value in money terms, which now includes money gains or losses due to the change in the value of money in the production and realization periods. Then, if we write the money markup as $*q$, and the value markup as q, we have:

$$*R(0) = R(0) = (1 + *q)*R'(0) = (1 + q)R'(0) \qquad (10.8)$$

The recovery of money costs corresponds to capital outlays in the past:

$$*R'(0) = \int_{-\infty}^{0} *C(t')a(t - t') \, \mathrm{d}t'$$

$$= a*(*g)\exp(-*gT) \qquad (10.9)$$

and similarly

$$R'(0) = a^*(g)\exp(-gT) \tag{10.10}$$

Thus we have

$$(1 + {}^*q)/(1 + q) = R'(0)/{}^*R'(0) = a^*(g)\exp(uT)/a^*(g + u) \tag{10.11}$$

where $u = {}^*g - g$, the difference between the rate of expansion of capital measured in money and the rate of expansion measured in labor value. The money markup exceeds the value markup by two factors, the change in the value of money during the production period, measured by the ratio of $a^*(g)$ to $a^*(g + u)$, and the change in the value of money during the realization period, measured by $\exp(uT) = \exp((g + u)T)/\exp(gT)$.

With this link we can move from the money accounting scheme to the value accounting scheme and back. The actual money rate of growth, ${}^*g$, will be determined by the money analog to (8.7):

$$1 = {}^*B(0) + \frac{c^*({}^*g)(1 + {}^*gp)[1 - k(1 - d^*({}^*g)) + {}^*B'(0)]}{1 + {}^*q(1 - (1-p)e^*({}^*g))} \tag{10.12}$$

The division of this rate of expansion between changes in the value of money and real accumulation are given by

$$u = u(T) \tag{10.13}$$

where T is determined by the money analog to (8.11c).

$$T = \frac{1}{g}\ln\left\{\frac{a^*({}^*g)(1 + {}^*g(1 - (1-p)e^*({}^*g)))}{1 - k(1 - d^*({}^*g)) + B'(0)}\right\} \tag{10.14}$$

With this method of treating changes in the value of money we have a system where the realized money rate of growth depends on the strength of aggregate demand. As this realized rate approaches the maximal rate of expansion of the system, a larger and large part of the monetary expansion takes the form of a depreciation in the value of money.

11. CREDIT AND INTEREST

The recommittal of money capital to production in the circuit of capital may take place directly, as in the cases of the recovery of capital outlays and the retention of profit by a capitalist firm, or indirectly, as in the case when a firm or household lends money realized in sales to another firm. This lending involves new forms of value, and of surplus value, although it changes nothing in the aggregate analysis of the preceding sections.

In a loan transaction an owner of money capital, the lender, places that money at the disposal of another agent, the borrower, under an enforceable agreement specifying how much money value the borrower will transfer back to the lender at particular future times or in particular future circumstances. If the total money value to be transferred back to the lender exceeds the amount lent, the difference is clearly a form of surplus value, called *interest*.

Loans and interest have probably existed in every society that has developed commodity relations and the money form of value. From the point of view of the labor theory of value, interest is always based on exploitation, since the lender receives command over social labor for which he has given no equivalent. This exploitation may be direct, in cases where the borrower pays the interest out of his or her own labor, like poor peasants who borrow to avoid starving in a bad year, or indirect, when the borrower pays the interest out of revenues derived from some other form of exploitation, like landowners who pay interest out of rents, or capitalists who pay interest out of profit.

In the context of the study of capitalist accumulation, the case of capitalist borrowing is of special significance. In this situation the motive of the capitalist in borrowing is not to ensure his physical survival, nor to alter his consumption pattern. The capitalist either wants to use the borrowed money as money capital in the circuit of capital to appropriate surplus values, or to ensure his economic survival by paying previous debts to avoid bankruptcy. Although borrowing by households to finance consumption and housing expenditures and by the State are quantitatively important in developed capitalist economies, it makes sense as a first step to focus our attention on specifically capitalist borrowing. The interest on loans made to capitalist firms is then ultimately a part of the surplus value appropriated when the loan is used as money capital to initiate capitalist production.

Marx expresses this by extending the diagram of the circuit of capital to include an original loan and the payment of principal and interest.

$$M^* - M - C\{(MP, LP)\dots(P)\dots C' - M' - M^{*'} \quad (11.1)$$

Here M^* is the money capital of the *financial capitalist*, which is lent to the *industrial capitalist*, passes through the circuit of capital and expands into M', and $M^{*'}$ is the payment of principal and interest (part of the surplus value) to the financial capitalist.

The "industrial" capitalist, or borrower, and the "financial" capitalist, or lender, are agents playing particular roles in a particular transaction. The same capitalist firm may find itself for one reason or another borrowing in one credit market and lending in another, thus performing the role of financial capitalist in one transaction, and the role of industrial capitalist in another. There is, of course, a tendency toward specialization of capitals in these roles.

The sequence of borrowing and lending may be layered even further because of the informational complexities of credit transactions. Agent A may lend to B, who, in turn, lends to the industrial capitalist, C, perhaps pooling A's funds with those of other lenders. This type of *financial intermediation* becomes highly developed in advanced capitalist societies. The intermediary takes some part of the interest paid by the ultimate borrower. Though intermediation adds greatly to the apparent complexity of financial arrangements, it does not fundamentally alter the source of capitalist interest in surplus value, nor the flows of value in the circuit of capital.

The level of the interest rate is determined by the bargain struck between borrowers and lenders as to what share of the surplus value appropriated through the use of a money capital will be returned to the lender. The analysis of this bargain rests on the nature of the agents involved, whether the marginal borrower and lender are capitalists, or worker or capitalist households, or the State. The central place of capitalist production and capital accumulation in capitalist society suggests that lending by capitalist firms to capitalist firms plays the dominant role in the formation of the interest rate. The problems of the theory of the level of the interest rate appear particularly sharply if we consider the case where there is no household or State borrowing or lending, so that all borrowers and lenders are capitalist firms.

If we abstract from the uncertainty of realization and the possibility of bankruptcy, capitalist firms would bid the interest rate to equality with the average rate of profit. No capitalist firm would lend for less than this, since it could use the funds in its own production to reap the average rate of profit, and no firm would borrow at a higher rate.

In reality, capitalist firms face uncertainty about their sales and face the risk of bankruptcy. At any moment different firms find themselves in different positions with regard to cash flow and the risk of bankruptcy. Some firms experience a shortage of money capital, and others a surplus. The interest rate is formed under these circumstances in the bargaining between the financially strong lenders and financially weak borrowers. Depending on how firms are distributed between these groups, the interest rate may be high or low relative to the average rate of profit (see Ref. 31, 32 on the concept of financial fragility).

These effects cannot be modeled directly in the circuit of capital framework, because they involve higher moments of the distribution of capitalist firms in the space of flows and stocks of value. The circuit of capital model, since it accounts for the social aggregate capital, reflects only changes in the first moment of these distributions.

The borrowing and lending of households and the State, if quantitatively large, can in this view influence the relation between the interest rate and the profit rate by changing the supply of loanable funds to capitalist firms. But since the financial position of the State and of households is largely determined by the circuit of capital, it would be a mistake to think of household or State behavior as fundamentally determining the interest rate (or through it the profit rate) as in neoclassical intertemporal equilibrium theories of the profit rate (as in Ref. 3 and 30).

The same factors that influence the level of the interest rate, the distribution of capitalist firms in the space of flows and stocks of value, also influence the average rate of spending on capital outlays for the system of capitals as a whole. Capitals that are in a weak financial position will conserve money capital by reducing the rate of their capital outlays as well as through borrowing. Capitals that are in a strong financial position will increase their capital outlays as well as their lending, other things being equal. But because the bankruptcy constraint is asymmetrical, a shift of the distribution of capitals toward financial weakness, even if the mean financial position of the aggregate capital is unchanged, will both raise the interest rate relative to the profit rate, and reduce the average rate of capital outlays. This effect is important in understanding the mechanism of crises in the accumulation process.

12. CENTRAL BANK POLICY

The Marxian view that sees the interest rate as the price of money capital within the framework of the circuit of capital is in sharp contrast to the Keynesian view that sees the interest rate as the price of liquidity. In particular, the Marxian view leads us to see central banks as regulating only a part of the spectrum of credit transactions. This in turn implies that central bank policy affects the *difference* between interest rates formed in unregulated markets ("the" interest rate of the last section) and interest rates offered borrowers and lenders by the financial intermediaries that are regulated by the central bank and influences by its policies. The central bank has no direct control over the average level of free market interest rates.

A simplified model of the banking system and central bank control, constructed so as to parallel standard Keynesian models as much as possible, may help to clarify these points.

In this model there are two ways for lending and borrowing to take place. First, lenders and borrowers may meet directly, without intermediation, and negotiate a loan contract at an interest rate r, the open market interest rate (which might be thought of as corresponding to the commercial paper rate in the U.S. financial system). Second, lenders may deposit their funds in banks at a deposit rate r_D. The banks then lend these funds to borrowers at the rate r_B. The banks' only liabilities are deposits, D (abstracting from the bank net worth account) and their assets are loans, L, and reserve deposits at the central bank, R. Assume that there is no hand-to-hand currency issued by the government, so that all transactions are paid by checks, and the quantity of money is just equal to the volume of bank deposits D. Suppose that banks are subject to a reserve requirement t, so that they must hold a fraction t of their deposits as reserves. Furthermore, assume that banks can lend and borrow reserves among themselves (as in the U.S. Federal Funds market) and that the interest rate formed in this market is r_F. The central bank creates reserves by buying direct placement loans, either those issued by private firms, or by the government, but does not lend directly to the banks, so that there is no interest rate in the model corresponding to the discount rate of the U.S. Federal Reserve System.

Suppose, then, that the cost to banks of servicing a loan is proportional to the size of the loan with the constant of proportionality c. Suppose further that, because of transaction costs experienced by some borrowers and lenders, deposits are not perfect substitutes for open market paper as assets for lenders, and bank loans are not perfect substitutes for open market paper to borrowers.

The direct cost to a bank of making a loan arises from its loss of reserves when the borrower uses the loan, since it will either lose the interest r_F it was earning on those reserves, or have to borrow reserves at the interest rate r_F, plus the cost of servicing the loan, c. Competition among banks in the loan market will force r_B to reflect these costs.

$$r_B = r_F + c \qquad (12.1)$$

If the reserve requirement is binding, banks will expand their loans and deposits by the familiar multiplier process until

$$R = tD \qquad (12.2)$$

Since the banks' balance sheets imply

$$D = R + L, \qquad (12.3)$$

we find

$$L = R((1/t) - 1) = aR \qquad (12.4)$$

where $a = ((1/t) - 1)$ is the bank loan multiplier.

The banks will be willing to expand to the limits set by reserves only if the rate they pay on deposits, r_D plus the direct cost of servicing deposits, d, is below their earnings on the excess reserves the deposit gives them.

$$r_D + d \leqslant r_F(1 - t) \tag{12.5}$$

Finally, the banks must compete with the open market. If F is the total flow of credit, then the ratio of bank lending and deposit rates to the open market rate r would depend on the size of bank lending and borrowing relative to the total.

$$r_B = g(L/F)r, \text{ with } g' < 0 \tag{12.6}$$

$$r_D = h(L/F)r, \text{ with } h' > 0 \tag{12.7}$$

The five equations (12.1)–(12.3), (12.6)–(12.7) determine the five variables D, L, r_B, r_D, r_F, given R, r, F, and t, as long as the inequality in (12.5) is satisfied. This solution implicitly assumes some limitation on the competition of banks for deposits, since if banks competed freely, (12.5) would have to hold with equality. This equality could be achieved by allowing d to become an endogenous variable, reflecting the costs banks would incur in competing for deposits.

In this model the central bank has control of the quantity of money through its control over the supply of reserves, but not over the open market interest rate, r, which could be determined by the factors discussed in the last section. The effect of changes in reserves is exhausted by changes in the market price of reserves, r_F, and by changes in the interest rate differential between bank loans and open market paper.

The Keynesian and monetarist models of this process abstract from the possibility of differences between bank lending rates and open market rates, and thus make it appear that the only way the system can adjust to an altered supply of reserves is through changes in the open market rate itself. The Keynesian and monetarist view essentially forces equality in (12.6), and introduces a demand for money function to determine the level of r.

13. PROPORTIONALITY IN SIMPLE AND EXPANDED REPRODUCTION

In Ref. 28, II, ch XXI, Marx sets out a model of *expanded reproduction*. His aim is to find conditions under which a capitalist economy could expand smoothly, assuming that it is not disturbed, as all real capitalist economies are, by changes in techniques of production and the value of labor-power. Two issues especially concern Marx in this analysis: first, the problem of realization, or the source of demand in such an economy, which we have treated in section 8 above; and second, the problem of the proper division of the social capital between the production of elements of constant capital, means of production (which Marx calls Department I) and production of the substance of variable capital, means of subsistence, (which Marx calls Department II).

Although this model is the starting point for the theory of consistent sectoral production planning (as in Leontiev's input-output analysis), Marx's conception differs from the sectoral models in important ways. Marx's Departments are not sectors, because they are defined with reference to the function their output plays in the expanded reproduction of capital, not by the physical characteristics of the output. The same output, structural steel, for example, may be partly used as means of production in building factories, and partly used as means of subsistence in building apartment houses. Thus the steel sector would be divided between Department I and Department II. Furthermore, the motive for a sectoral division of production in an input-output table is primarily to understand the *technical* requirements of achieving a certain production plan. Marx's division corresponds to the division of capital as value between constant and variable capital, a distinction that arises specifically from the labor theory of value. Thus Marx's motive is to understand the *social* conditions for the reproduction of capital. The technical requirements reflected in the input-output table apply to any system of social production, but the division between constant and variable capital, and hence the distinction between Departments I and II reflects a specifically capitalist organization of social production.

We can treat this problem by using the methods already

developed to study the aggregate circuit of capital in section 7 above separately for each Department. We will allow each Department to have its own lag functions for production and finance, its own capitalization rate, composition of capital outlays, and rate of exploitation (to allow for possible deviations of price from value) and hence its own markup.

Two new issues are raised by the division of capital between the two Departments. First, if markups, time lags, and capitalization rates differ between the Departments, it is not certain that they will both be capable of growing at the same exponential rate when each Department finances its expansion out of its own surplus value. Marx handles this problem by adjusting the capitalization rates in the two Departments [28] II, p. 512 so as to be consistent. The other approach to this problem would be to allow borrowing and lending between the two Departments at an interest rate equal to a common profit rate.

This second approach is closer to the institutional reality of modern capital accumulation, but it leads to some unhappy analytical outcomes. If capitalists in Department I, for example, have a higher capitalization rate, so that they accumulate more value than is necessary to finance Department I accumulation, and lend the surplus to Department II, they will gradually come to own the whole social capital. The social capitalization rate would converge over time to the Department I capitalization rate. Because these effects are tangential to the problem of proportionality in reproduction, we will assume that the profit rates and capitalization rates in the two Departments are the same, and that each Department finances its own expansion.

Second, we now face the question of equalizing output and the social demand for output in each Department separately. This problem Marx tried to solve numerically in his schemes of reproduction [28] II, ch XXI.

To simplify the analysis, assume also that households and the State have no spending lags and do not borrow.

If we rewrite (7.4), (7.5) and (8.7) separately for each Department, we have (suppressing the Department subscripts)

$$P(0) = (1 + q)a^*(g)C(0) \qquad (13.1)$$

$$R(0) = (1 + q)a^*(g)b^*(g)C(0) \tag{13.2a}$$

$$R'(0) = a^*(g)b^*(g)C(0) \tag{13.2b}$$

$$R''(0) = qa^*(g)b^*(g)C(0) \tag{13.2c}$$

$$C(0) = (R'(0) + pR''(0))c^*(g)C(0) + B(0)$$
$$= (1 + pq)a^*(g)b^*(g)c^*(g)C(0) + B(0) \tag{13.3}$$

The demand for Department I's output arises from the constant capital outlays of the two Departments. The demand for Department II's output arises from the variable capital outlays of the Departments and capitalist consumption out of surplus value. In each Department, this demand must be the value actually realized on a consistent path of expanded reproduction.

$$D_I = (1 - k_I)C_I(0) + (1 - k_{II})C_{II}(0)$$
$$= R_I(0) \tag{13.4a}$$

$$D_{II} = (k_I C_I(0) + k_{II}C_{II}(0) + (1 - p)(R_I(0) + R_{II}(0))$$
$$= R_{II}(0) \tag{13.4b}$$

Furthermore, on a path of expanded reproduction,

$$g_I = g_{II} = g \tag{13.5}$$

since the two Departments must expand at the same rate.

If we sum (13.4a) and (13.4b) and use (13.5), we get one condition that links the growth rate g and the relative sizes of the two Departments, as expressed by the ratio of each capital outlay to the total.

$$1 = (1 + pq_I)a_I^*(g)b_I^*(g)[(C_I(0)/C(0)]$$
$$+ (1 + pq_{II})(a_{II}^*(g)b_{II}^*(g)[C_{II}(0)/C(0)] \tag{13.6}$$

We can also solve (13.4a) directly to get a second relation linking the growth rate g and the relative sizes of the two Departments as expressed by the ratio of their capital outlays.

$$\frac{C_I(0)}{C_{II}(0)} = \frac{1 - k_{II}}{(1 + q_I)a_I^*(g)b_I^*(g) - (1 - k_I)} \tag{13.7}$$

These two equations together jointly determine g and the ratio

$C_I(0)/C_{II}(0)$, and hence, assuming that $C(0) = C_I(0) + C_{II}(0) = 1$, $C_I(0)$ and $C_{II}(0)$.

Equation (13.3) then serves to determine the borrowing levels in each Department required to sustain expanded reproduction.

Equation (13.7) has several important special cases. Suppose, first, that we are studying simple reproduction, so that $p_I = p_{II} = 0$, and the growth rate g is also 0. Then equation (8.10) becomes

$$\frac{C_I(0)}{C_{II}(0)} = \frac{1 - k_{II}}{q_I + k_I} \tag{13.8}$$

or

$$(q_I + k_I)C_I(0) = (1 - k_{II})C_{II}(0) \tag{13.9}$$

If we translate equation (13.9) back into Marx's notation, we see that it says that the sum of surplus value and variable capital in Department I must equal the constant capital in Department II. This is Marx's basic result in the analysis of simple reproduction. Department I reproduces its own constant capital, so that the rest of the value of its product, equal to its variable capital plus surplus value, must take the form of the constant capital necessary for Department II.

$$s_I + v_I = c_{II} \tag{13.10}$$

But equation (13.7) also tells us the necessary proportions to maintain expanded reproduction in both Departments.

Marx implicitly treats the problem of expanded reproduction as a period model, with periods that he refers to as "years". Capital outlays take place at the beginning of a year, and production is completed within the year. The product is realized at the beginning of the next year by the sale of the output. In the notation that we have been using, $C_I(t)$ is capital outlays at the beginning of year t, $Q_I(t)$ is the flow of finished product at the end of year t valued at its cost of production, and $R_I(t)$ is the sales at the beginning of year t, all for Department I, and similarly for Department II. Marx's assumptions in working out his schema of reproduction are

$$Q(t) = C(t) \tag{13.11}$$

$$R(t) = (1 + q)Q(t - 1) \tag{13.12}$$

$$C(t) = R'(t) + pR''(t) \tag{13.13}$$

for each Department. The balance condition he proposes is that the output of Department I be realized through the capital outlays for constant capital in the two Departments.

$$R_I(t) = (1 - k_I)C_I(t) + (1 - k_{II})C_{II}(t) \tag{13.14}$$

Marx's system is a set of difference equations, but a comparison of (13.11)–(13.14) with (13.1)–(13.14) shows that they are exactly the same as the circuit of capital equations, with simple time delay lags, where the time delays are $T_P = T_F = 0$ and $T_R = 1$. Thus (13.7) also gives the necessary initial conditions for balanced growth in Marx's schemas. Since $(1 + pq) = \exp(g)$ (for either Department), we can write (13.7) as

$$\frac{C_I(0)}{C_{II}(0)} = \frac{(1 - K_{II})(1 + p_I q_I)}{(1 + q_I) - (1 - k_I)(1 + p_I q_I)} \tag{13.15}$$

The significance of (13.15) in terms of Marx's schemas is simple. If one begins with the capitals in the two Departments in the proportions indicated by (13.15), it is possible for the system to continue smoothly along a path of balanced expanded reproduction. If one starts with any different proportions, it will be impossible to meet all the conditions for expanded reproduction. For example, consider Marx's first attempt to develop a consistent schema of expanded reproduction [28] II, pp 505 ff. He sets up the following tableau:

	c	v	s	$c + v + s$
I	4,000	1,000	1,000	6,000
II	1,500	376	376	2,252

Marx assumes that each Department converts half its surplus value into capital, so that, in the circuit of capital notation, $p_I = p_{II} = 1/2$. He apparently wants to have the same composition of capital $k_I = k_{II} = 0.2$ in both Departments, though to achieve this the variable capital and surplus value in Department II ought to be 375, not 376. The rate of exploitation is the same, 1, in each Department, so that they have the same markups, $q_I = q_{II} = 0.2$.

If we follow Marx in trying to follow through the consequences of these assumptions, we find that the demand for the output of Department I consists of the replacement of its own constant capital, the replacement of Department II's constant capital, and the provision of additional constant capital to allow each Department to expand its operations in the original proportions. This demand is

$$c_I + c_{II} + p_I(1 + k_I)s_I + p_{II}(1 - k_{II})s_{II} =$$
$$4{,}000 + 1{,}500 + 400 + 150 \qquad\qquad = 6{,}050$$

which is 50 more than the actual output of Department I in the tableau. A similar calculation shows that the demand for the output of Department II is 50 too small. The discrepancy annoyed Marx, and he devotes several pages of his notes to trying to find a schema that will exhibit proportional expanded reproduction.

We can see what is wrong if we use equation (13.15). If we use the parameters assumed by Marx in equation (13.15) we can see that the proper ratio of C_I to C_{II} is 2.75 to permit balanced expanded reproduction. Marx's initial ratio, however, is $5{,}000/1{,}875 = 2.6667$, which is not equal to 2.75. If Marx had started with a capital of 1818.18 in Department II, instead of 1975, he would have found that the balancing conditions were satisfied.

Thus the general conditions for proportionality in expanded reproduction is given by (13.6) and (13.7). These results complete the discussion of the problems raised by Marx in his study of expanded reproduction.

14. ACCUMULATION

Accumulation in real capitalist economies does not resemble the models of expanded reproduction very closely. We see an uneven pattern of historical accumulation, marked by crises of aggregate demand, chronic emergence of disproportionality, and continual changes in the underlying parameters of capital accumulation.

Real accumulation, then, is not just a quantitative increase in the scale of production, but a continuing process of qualitative change, as new techniques and products emerge, and the sociological context of the economic system is transformed. From Marx's point of view, many of the changes that conventional economic theory sees as external shocks to the economy are in fact the systematic consequencies of the accumulation of capital.

These qualitative changes are reflected quantitatively in changes in the underlying parameters of the circuit of capital. The real process of capital accumulation, then, must be represented by a non-linear model in which the parameters of the circuit of capital depend explicitly on the path of capital accumulation. Such models are, of course, considerably less tractable to mathematical analysis than the linear models we have developed up to this point.

Considerable importance also attaches to what the specific non-linearities are, and what are their relative importances. Take, for example, the "Pigou effect", the contention that the level of consumption spending will rise, other things being equal, if the "real" value of household money balances increases through price deflation. In the context of the circuit of capital, this idea must link household money balances, the value of money, the spending lags of worker and capitalist households, and the captalization rate. In a similar fashion, many of Keynes' claims about critical aspects of the dynamics of income determination translate into non-linearities in the circuit of capital framework. The notion of liquidity preference, to take another example, must refer to a dependence of capital spending lags on the relation between the interest rate and the profit rate.

Marx himself put forward several conjectures about the importance of non-linearities in real capital accumulation. The most famous of these is the interconnected set of ideas associated with the "tendency for the rate of profit to fall" with capital accumulation. This nexus of ideas (among which the actual fall in the rate of profit may be the least important) is Marx's characteristic contribution to our understanding of the essential nature of capitalist economic systems.

Marx's central idea is that capitalism, as a technically progressive mode of production, exhibits a characteristic profile in the historical development of the parameters of the circuit of capital. Capital accumulation, in Marx's vision, starts with the transformation of relatively unproductive labor processes inherited from other forms of production into capitalist production. Because of the low productivity of these processes the surplus labor time available from them is small. In terms of the circuit of capital model this corresponds to a relatively high level of the value of labor-power and consequently a low rate of surplus value, e. On the other hand, these techniques require relatively small amounts of means of production and have short production periods. Thus the composition of capital outlays, k, is high, and the production time lag short. We might speculate that the rapid turnover of productive capital in the early stages of capitalist development was offset by relatively slow turnover of commercial and money capital. The markup and the limiting rate of profit could be quite high under these circumstances, because of the high level of the composition of capital outlays, despite the low rate of surplus value.

Capital itself, in its pursuit of surplus value, will revolutionize the processes of production to achieve higher levels of labor productivity and hence higher rates of surplus value. But, Marx argues, this technical progress must systematically tend to lower the composition of capital outlays, and lower the turnover of productive capital as more massive and longer-lived means of production come into use. This argument does not claim that every innovation must lower the composition of capital outlays, but does require a tendency for this fall to take place on average over time. Thus Marx expected to find higher levels of labor productivity, higher rates of surplus value, and lower compositions of capital and longer turnover times for productive capital after a significant period of capital accumulation. We might suspect that the turnover of commercial and money capital might be accelerated by this same process of development. Marx argued that this nexus of developments, by which capitalist production defeats diminishing returns to fixed resources through technical change, provides a rational explanation for the tendency of the profit rate to fall with capital accumulation. The lower composition of capital outlays and slower turnover of productive capital could outweigh the rise in rates of surplus value. Marx found this analysis particularly attractive compared to what he viewed as Ricardo's irrational attempt to explain falling rates of profit as a reflection of diminishing returns, thereby obscuring what Marx viewed as the essential character of capitalist production, its technical progressiveness (see also Ref. 19).

There is little doubt that several of the elements of this conception do describe pervasive historical tendencies of capital accumulation (see Ref. 8, 9, 17, 29, 50 and 51). No one disputes the claim that capitalism is a technically progressive mode of production, nor that an essential dynamic in capitalist development is a growth of labor productivity more rapid than the growth of the real wage. It is easy to demonstrate empirically that the average composition of capital outlays, k, has fallen over long historical periods, though the evidence on the rates of turnover of capital is less reliable and less clear-cut. There is also reason to believe that the average rate of profit has fallen over long epochs of capital accumulation, though this fall seems to have been reversed in periods of extremely rapid technical progress like the Second World War and its aftermath.

Considerable attention (see for example Ref. 36, 43, 55) has been focussed on the analytical finding that if capitalist firms adopt only new techniques that raise profits at existing prices, and real wages remain constant in a completely closed economic system, then capitals will never adopt new techniques that lower the system-wide average rate of profit. From a practical point of view this result is not of much relevance. Real capital accumulation involves a rising real wage, even as it generally leads to a rising rate of exploitation. If labor productivity is rising, workers may be able to produce a higher standard of living for themselves with shorter labor times. Marx's own argument acknowledges this by taking (in his discussion of the tendency of the rate of profit to fall) the value of labor-power, and not the real wage, as constant.

If one holds the value of labor-power (that is, the wage share of value added) constant, then there are viable techniques that lower costs at existing prices but which lead to lower general rates of profit when they are universally adopted. It is possible to exhibit examples of this in a one-commodity model of production. Suppose production of one unit of the commodity initially requires a units of the commodity and n units of labor, that capital turns over completely in one period, and that labor is paid at the beginning of the period at a money wage w. Assume also that the value of money is 1, so that one unit of money is equivalent to one unit of labor time. Then the labor value (and price) of the commodity will be

$$v = n + av \tag{14.1}$$

or

$$v = n/(1 - a) \tag{14.1a}$$

The equilibrium rate of profit will be

$$r = \frac{v - av - wn}{av + wn} = \frac{(1 - w)n}{(a/(1 - a) + w)n} = \frac{(1 - w)}{(a/(1 - a) + w)} \tag{14.2}$$

Clearly any new technique that raises a will lower the equilibrium rate of profit, holding the money wage and the value of money, and hence the value of labor-power, constant. But the viable, cost reducing, techniques, given w and v are those for which

$$va' + wn' < va + wn \tag{14.3}$$

Among these there will obviously be some for which $a' > a$, as long as

$$\frac{a' - a}{1 - 1'} < \frac{w}{v} \tag{14.4}$$

In this example we have held the value of labor-power constant by stipulating that the value of money is 1 unit of labor time per monetary unit, and holding the money wage constant. The Okishio method would assume a constant real wage b, so that

$$\frac{w}{v} = b \tag{14.5}$$

in equilibrium. In this case the equilibrium rate of profit can be written

$$r = \frac{v - av - wn}{av + wn} = \frac{v(1 - a - bn)}{v(a + bn)} = \frac{1 - (a + bn)}{a + bn} \quad (14.6)$$

In this case any alternative technique (a', n') such that

$$va' + wn' = v(a' + bn') < v(a + bn) \quad (14.7)$$

has

$$a' + bn' < a + bn \quad . \quad (14.8)$$

and this must raise the equilibrium rate of profit, as the Okishio argument claims.

The critique of the theory of the tendency of the rate of profit to fall based on the Okishio theorem is perhaps a fair rejoinder to Marx, who was extremely reluctant to admit explicitly that rising labor productivity with a constant value of labor-power implies a rising real wage. This same critique, on the other hand, is of little relevance to our understanding of the historical evolution of real capitalist economies, which generally exhibit a rising real wage and a falling value of labor-power (or rising rate of surplus value). Thus the real economies fall into the class of cases where the movement of the rate of profit cannot be predicted on a priori theoretical grounds.

The behavior of the rate of profit in the short and long period is one of the most important non-linear phenomena in the accumulation process. Careful studies of this non-linearity are a crucial element in a research program for understanding the dynamics of capital accumulation.

15. ECONOMIC CRISIS

Real capital accumulation, in sharp contrast to the fiction of expanded reproduction, is marked by periods of economic crisis. These crises begin with symptoms of overrapid expansion of the economy: rising money prices of commodities, shortages of certain commodities and certain types of labor-power, and high interest rates. The economy then reaches a turning point at which aggregate demand and output turn down sharply, and the demand for labor-power falls. The interest rate is very high relative to rates of profit at the turning point, and prices often continue to rise in many sectors for some time after the turning point. Output, profits, and employment continue to fall for some time, usually followed by a substantial decline in the rate of price increase and a fall in the level of interest rates relative to profit rates. The decline sooner or later comes to an end and the accumulation process resumes its upward course (see Ref. 34).

The length of the different phases of these periodic crises and the amplitudes of the motions are far from regular. There is no apparent relation between the length of one phase and that of succeeding ones, nor between the magnitude of contractions and succeeding expansions. Despite the fascination of macroeconomists with linear difference and differential equations which have cyclic modes among their solutions (see for example Ref. 45), the instabilities of capital accumulation do not seem to have the characteristics of physical linear oscillators.

Marx views capitalist crisis as an historic phenomenon in the sense that each crisis manifests the maturing of the particular contradictions of a particular wave of accumulation. The accumulation process is seen as poisoning itself by gradually destroying its own preconditions. In the circuit of capital framework, this idea can be expressed as systematic changes in the underlying parameters of the accumulation process, the markup, capitalization rate, and time lags in production, realization, and finance. These changes in parameters must force the system off its path of steady expansion (see Ref. 49, 57 and 58).

In mathematical terms, this type of explanation of crisis involves studying the non-linear relations among the parameters of the circuit of capital and between those parameters and capital accumulation itself. This is not an easy analytical task, and is made more difficult because the range of possible non-linearities is very large, and empirical exploration of them very tentative.

Furthermore, it seems likely that the exploration of these problems will require a shift from the study of aggregates, or averages, as in the present formulations of this model, to an explicit representation of the ensemble of individual capitals. Such a representation would allow for the analysis of higher moments of key distributions describing this ensemble (in terms of balance sheet stocks and income statement flows) than the means studied in the aggregate circuit of capital. Pending the development of such a theory the discussion of capitalist crisis must remain at the level of conjecture.

It is possible, however, to develop a quasi-dynamic analysis of the circuit of capital model which shows the reaction of that model to single shocks in the basic parameters.

Suppose that we study the circuit of capital model as described in section 8, assuming that the basic parameters of the model have had constant values, $p_0, q_0, a_0(), c_0(), d_0(), e_0(), B_0, B'_0, g_0$ up to time zero and that the system suddenly shifts to a new parameter set $p, q, a(), c(), c(), d(), e(), B, B', g$ at time zero. The new path of borrowing must be consistent with the new steady state growth rate; in other words the new parameter set must satisfy (8.7c) and (8.11d).

The paths of the variables from time zero onward will be determined, first, by what is left "in the pipeline" as a result of capital outlays made before time zero, and, second, by the dynamic interactions of the new parameters after time zero. The path of the system up to time zero constitutes a set of initial conditions for its motion after time zero.

We can write the basic equations for capital outlays, realization (assuming no gold production) and value of output as follows:

$$C(t) = \int_0^t (R'(t') + pR''(t'))c(t - t') \, dt' + B(t)$$

$$+ \int_{-\infty}^0 (R'(t') + p_0R''(t'))c_0(t - t') \, dt' \qquad (15.1)$$

$$R(t) = D(t) = (1 - k)C(t) + \int_0^t kC(t')d(t - t') \, dt' \quad (15.2)$$

$$+ \int_0^t (1 - p)R''(t7)e(t - t') \, dt' + B'(t)$$

$$+ \int_{-\infty}^{0} k_0 C(t') d_0(t - t') \, dt'$$

$$+ \int_{-\infty}^{0} (1 - p_0) R''(t') e_0(t - t') \, dt' \qquad (15.2)$$

$$P(t) = (1 + q) \int_{0}^{t} C(t') a(t - t') \, dt'$$

$$+ (1 + q_0) \int_{-\infty}^{0} C(t') a_0(t - t') \, dt' \qquad (15.3)$$

The paths of the other variables, including the stocks of value in financial, productive, and commercial capital, and the realization time lag, can be recovered once we know the paths of these basic variables.

It is convenient to express the solution of these equations in the form of Laplace transforms, using the assumption that, up to time zero, the variables all follow exponential paths at the common growth rate g_0. The initial conditions terms (those with integral limits from $-\infty$ to 0) all have the same form, an exponential function convoluted with a transfer function. The transform of such expressions can be illustrated by working out the simplest equation, (15.3).

If $P^*(s)$ is the Laplace transform of $P(t)$, defined by

$$P^*(s) = \int_{0}^{t} \exp(-st) P(t) \, dt \qquad (15.4)$$

with the property that the transform of convolutions is equal to the product of the transforms of the convoluted functions, we have, from (15.3)

$$P^*(s) = (1 + q) a^*(s) C^*(s)$$

$$+ (1 + q_0) \int_{0}^{\infty} \exp(-st) \int_{-\infty}^{\infty} \exp(g_0 t') a_0(t - t') \, dt' \, dt \qquad (15.5)$$

The integral in this equation can be simplified by letting $t'' = t - t'$, and the result is

$$P^*(s) = (1 + q) a^*(s) C^*(s) + (1 + q_0) \frac{a_0{}^*(g_0) - a_0{}^*(s)}{s - g_0} \qquad (15.6)$$

since the transform of an exponential growing at rate g is just $1/(s-g)$.

By similar manipulations we find

$$C^*(s) = c^*(s)[R'^*(s) + pR''^*(s)] + B^*(s)$$

$$+ [R'(0) + p_0 R''(0)] \frac{[c_0^*(g_0) - c_0^*(s)]}{s - g_0} \qquad (15.7)$$

$$R^*(s) = (1-k)C^*(s) + kd^*(s)C^*(s) + (1-p)e^*(s)R''^*(s) + B'^*(s)$$

$$+ \frac{k_0[d_0^*(g_0) - d_0^*(s)]}{s - g_0}$$

$$+ \frac{(1-p_0)R''(0)[e_0^*(g_0) - e_0^*(s)]}{s - g_0} \qquad (15.8)$$

The reader can verify that if none of the parameters change, continued exponential growth at rate g_0 is a solution to these equations.

If one or more of the parameters do change, the flows of value will undergo a transient motion before converging to the new steady state path at growth rate g.

In this general model a difficulty arises from the necessity of distinguishing the two components of realization, R', the recovery of capital outlays, and R'', the realization of surplus value. If the markup changes at time zero, the proportions of surplus value and recovery of capital outlays in sales will not change until the vintage zero output passes through the sales lag and is actually sold. Since the sales lag, T, will vary in the transient motion, this introduces a non-linearity into the process. In order to avoid this complication, we will confine our analysis to the case where $p = p_0 = 1$, so that all surplus value is reinvested. With this assumption, (15.7) and (15.8) become

$$C^*(s) = c^*(s)R^*(s) + B^*(s)$$

$$+ \frac{R(0)[c_0^*(g_0) - c_0^*(s)]}{s - g_0} \qquad (15.9)$$

$$R^*(s) = (1 - k(1 - d^*(s))C^*(s) + B'^*(s)$$
$$+ \frac{k_0[d_0^*(g_0) - d_0^*(s)]}{s - g_0} \qquad (15.10)$$

These two equations can be solved to give the transform of the transient path after the parameter change at time zero. The expression for $C^*(s)$ is, for example,

$$C^*(s) = [(s - g_0)(c^*(s)B'^*(s) + B^*(s))$$
$$+ c^*(s)k_0(d_0^*(g_0) - d_0^*(s))$$
$$+ R(0)(c_0^*(g_0) - c_0^*(s))]]$$
$$[s - g_0][1 - (1 - k(1 - d^*(s)))c^*(s)] \qquad (15.11)$$

The transient motion of the capital outlays can be recovered from this transform, and the motion of the other stock and flow variables can be derived from it.

For example, to simplify let us assume that workers spend their wages instantly, so that $d^*(s) = 1$, that the spending lag $c()$ is an exponential lag with parameter c ($c(t) = c\exp(-ct)$), so that $c^*(s) = c/(s + c)$, that $B'(t) = 0$, and that $B(t)$ after time zero is equal to $B(0)\exp(gt)$ where g is the new steady state accumulation rate, given, from (8.7c) by

$$g = \frac{c}{1 - B(0)} - c = \frac{cB(0)}{1 - B(0)} \qquad (15.12)$$

Under these assumptions $R(0) = 1$, from (8.6) so that

$$C^*(s) = \frac{(s - g_0)B^*(s) + [c_0^*(g_0) - c_0^*(s)]}{(s - g_0)(1 - c^*(s))}$$
$$= \frac{g(s + c)}{(g + c)s(s - g)} + \frac{c_0(s + c)}{(g_0 + c_0)s(s + c_0)} \qquad (15.13)$$

using the fact that $B^*(s) = g/[(g + c)(s - g)]$ and simplifying.

First note that only the growth rate and the spending lag appear in this expression. A fall in the markup, as we have seen already in section 8, if the path of borrowing remains unchanged, will not affect the growth rate, but will be absorbed by changes in inventories of finished commodities as reflected by the realization lag T.

Using the method of residues, or expanding the fractions in (15.13) directly, we can write the time path of $C(t)$ as

$$C(t) = \exp(gt) - \frac{c - c_0}{g_0 + c_0} \exp(-c_0 t) + c\left(\frac{1}{g_0 + c_0} - \frac{1}{g + c}\right)$$

$$+ \frac{c[(g - g_0) + (c - c_0)]}{(g_0 + c_0)(g + c)} \quad (15.14)$$

so that

$$C(0) = 1 + \frac{c_0 g - c g_0}{(g_0 + c_0)(g + c)} \quad (15.15)$$

Capital outlays, C, jump upward or downward at time zero depending on whether $c_0/c > < g_0/g$, and then smoothly converge to the new steady state path. Thus a crisis-like motion, involving a fall in capital outlays and output, could be the result of either a fall in the rate of borrowing, or a rise in the capitalist spending lag (which corresponds to a fall in the parameter c). A fall in the markup would produce such a crisis only through its effects on the spending lag $c()$ or on the path of new borrowing $B()$.

It is thus possible to get some insights into the dynamic behavior of circuit of capital models with these methods.

16. CONCLUSION

The investigation of Marx's conception of the circuit of capital reveals important connections between money, accumulation, and capitalist crisis.

Within the framework of the circuit of capital we can see the integral role money capital plays in the reproduction and expansion of capitalist production. We also see that the provision of financial assets is itself an incident in the circuit of capital. This places the role of the monetary policy of the central bank in a subordinate place. It also suggests that disturbances in the financial system reflect disturbances in capital accumulation.

Furthermore, because there is a close connection between the scale of capital outlays, aggregate demand, and new borrowing, it seems likely that the financial system plays a crucial role in transforming changes in the underlying parameters of accumulation like the markup into crises. Without feedback through financial variables to capital outlays there is no reason why the system could not adapt smoothly and gradually to a lower markup without a crisis. This suggests further that the persistence of crises depends strongly on the persistence of financial imbalance that have grown during periods of accumulation (see Ref. 32).

These conclusions have important ramifications for the Marxist theory of crises. Classical Marxism argued that capitalist crises were rooted in the fundamentally contradictory character of the capitalist mode of production. Thus it is impossible to avoid crises as long as production remains organized on capitalist principles. Furthermore, classical Marxism taught that crises would worsen as the contradictions of capitalism matured, leading to a final or ultimate crisis in which a revolutionary transformation of capitalism would become unavoidable.

Capitalist crisis certainly reflects the contradiction between exchange value and use value on which commodity production systems rest, since it exhibits a simultaneous increase of unfilled need and of unused capacity to meet need. Crises are inherent in a system where the proximate motive for production is surplus value, and the meeting of need is achieved as a contingent byproduct of the pursuit of profit. This analysis cannot, however, support the conclusion that the capitalist mode of production is contradictory in the sense of posing logically inconsistent requirements for its own reproduction, of being, in fact impossible. Crisis must be seen as part of the normal pattern of successful reproduction of capitalism.

Finance appears to be a critical mediating channel between changes in underlying parameters of accumulation like the markup and the ebbing of aggregate demand associated with the realization phase of crises. The disruption of the financial system is itself one of the most dramatic manifestations of such crises. But the circuit of capital analysis tends to confirm the view that financial problems have their origin in systematic effects of capital accumulation. Crises are not primarily financial, and no reform of the financial system alone can eliminate the tendency to crisis.

The circuit of capital models suggest, however, a much wider spectrum of effects of crisis than those identified by classical Marxism. The possibility that a fall in the markup might lead to higher rates of price inflation, rather than to a classic recessionary downturn, depending on the financial system and its behavior, is one example.

Furthermore, if the persistence and severity of crises depend on the persistence of financial imbalances, there are presumably strong state measures available to avoid systemic catastrophe. The financial system is a system of promises, and a financial crisis is a situation where a large number of such promises cannot be met consistently. If the state can achieve an orderly dissolution of enough financial promises, it can create a situation where accumulation can proceed, as long as there is a surplus value potentially available in the unpaid labor of productive workers.

This last remark calls into serious question the idea of a final or ultimate crisis of capitalist production arising purely from the predictable effects of accumulation. Economic crises may become more severe in their social impact as larger parts of the population depend on capitalist production to meet a larger part of their need. But if social labor is capable of producing a surplus, it is hard to see why a society that agreed on capitalist principles could not arrange to have that potential surplus take the form of a surplus value.

The investigation of problems within the circuit of capital framework has been only slightly developed. In particular, the study of systems with an ensemble of capitals distributed in the space of balance sheet and income statement variables is likely to provide a large number of important problems that can be attacked with modern statistical and modelling methods.

Barnard College, Columbia University

REFERENCES

*1. Aglietta, N. *A Theory of Capitalist regulation: The U.S. Experience*. London: NLB, 1979.
2. Clower, R. W. The foundations of monetary theory, *Western Economic Journal*, **6 (1969), 1–9, reprinted in *Monetary Theory*, ed. by R. W. Clower. Harmondsworth: Penguin, 1969.

**3. Debreu, G. *Theory of Value: An Axiomatic Analysis of Economic Equilibrium*. New Haven: Yale University Press, 1959.

*4. deBrunhoff, S. *Marx on Money*. New York: Urizen, 1976.

**5. deVroey, M.: "Value, Production and Exchange" in *The Value Controversy*. London: Verso and NLB, 1981.

6. Domar, E. "Capital Expansion, Rate of Growth, and Employment", *Econometrica*, **14 (1946), 137–147.

*7. Dumenil, G.: *De la Valeur aux Prix de Production*. Paris: Economica, 1980.

8. Dumenil, G. and M. Glick: "La Basse de la Rentabilite Aux Etats Unis: Inventaire de Recherches et Mise en Perspective Historique", *Observations et Diagnostics Economiques*, **6 (January 1984), 69–92.

**9. Dumenil, G. and M. Glick: "The Tendency of the Rate of Profit to Fall in the United States", *Contemporary Marxism*, forthcoming, 1984.

*10. Fine, B. and L. Harris: *Rereading Capital*. New York: Columbia University Press, 1979.

*11. Foley, D. K.: "The Value of Money, the Value of Labor Power, and the Marxian Transformation Problem", *Review of Radical Political Economics*, **14** (2) (1982), 37–47.

12. Foley, D. K.: "Realization and Accumulation in a Marxian Model of the Circuit of Capital", *Journal of Economic Theory*, **28(2) (1982) 300–319.

**13. Foley, D. K.: "Say's Law in Marx and Keynes", *Cahiers d'Economie Politique*, forthcoming.

**14. Friedman, M.: *A Theory of the Consumption Function*. Princeton: Princeton University Press, 1957.

15. Garegnani, P.: "Heterogenous Capital, the Production Function, and the Theory of Distribution", *Review of Economic Studies*, **37 (1970), 407–436.

16. Gerstein, I.: "Domestic Work and Capitalism", *Radical America*, **7 (4 and 5) (1973).

**17. Gillman, J. M.: *The Falling Rate of Profit*. New York: Cameron Associates, 1957.

18. Harris, D. J.: "On Marx's Scheme of Reproduction and Accumulation", *Journal of Political Economy*, 80 (1972), 505–522, reprinted in *The Economics of Marx*, ed. by M. C. Howard and J. E. King. Harmondsworth: Penguin, 1976.

**19. Harris, D. J.: "Are There Macroeconomic Laws? The Law of the Falling Rate of Profit Reconsidered", in *The Economic Law of Motion of Modern Society: A Marx-Keynes-Schumpeter Centennial*, ed. by M. J. Wagener and J. W. Drukker. Cambridge: Cambridge University Press, 1984.

**20. Harrod, R.: *Towards a Dynamic Economics*. London: Macmillan, 1948.

21. Himmelweit, S. and S. Mohun: "Domestic Labour and Capital", *Cambridge Journal of Economics*, **1(1) (1977), 15–32.

*22. Kalecki, M.: *Studies in the Theory of Business Cycles*. New York: Kelley, 1969.

*23. Keynes, J. M.: *The General Theory of Employment, Interest, and Money*. New York: Harcourt, Brace and World, 1964.

**24. Leontiev, W.: *The Structure of the American Economy*, 2nd edition. New York: Oxford University Press, 1951.

25. Lipietz, A.: "The So-Called 'Transformation Problem' Revisited", *Journal of Economic Theory*, **26 (1982), 59–88.

**26. Luxemburg, R.: *The Accumulation of Capital*. New York: Modern Reader, 1968.

**27. Luxemburg, R.: *The Accumulation of Capital, an Anti-Critique*, and Bukharin, N. *Imperialism and the Accumulation of Capital*. New York: Monthly Review, 1972.

*28. Marx, K.: *Capital*, Volumes I, II, III. New York: International Publishers, 1967.

**29. Mage, S.: "The 'Law of the Tendency of the Falling Rate of Profit': its Place in the Marxian Theoretical System and Relevance to the U.S. Economy, 1900–1960", Ph.D dissertation, Columbia University, 1963.

**30. Malinvaud, E.: *Lectures on Microeconomic Theory*. North-Holland, 1976.

*31. Minsky, H.: *John Maynard Keynes*. New York: Columbia University Press, 1975.

**32. Minsky, H.: *Can it Happen Again?* New York: M. E. Sharpe, 1982.

33. Modigliani, F.: "The Life-Cycle Hypothesis of Saving, the Demand for Wealth, and the Supply of Capital", *Social Research* **33(2) (1966), 160–217.

*34. Moore, G. H.: *Business Cycles, Inflation, and Forecasting*, 2nd edition. Cambridge, Massachusetts: NBER, Ballinger, 1983.

**35. Niehans, J.: *The Theory of Money*. Baltimore: Johns Hopkins University Press, 1978.

*36. Okishio, N.: "Technical Change and the Rate of Profit", *Kobe University Economic Review* **7** (1961), 86–99.

37. Ostroy, J. and R. M. Starr: "Money and the Decentralization of Exchange", *Econometrica*, **42(6) (1974), 1093–1113.

*38. Pasinetti, L.: *Growth and Income Distribution: Essays in Economic Theory*. Cambridge: Cambridge University Press, 1974.

*39. Pasinetti, L.: *Lectures in the Theory of Production*. New York: Columbia University Press, 1977.

**40. Patinkin, D.: *Money, Interest and Prices*, 2nd Edition. New York: Harper and Row, 1965.

*41. Ricardo, D.: *Principles of Political Economy and Taxation*. Harmondsworth: Penguin, 1971.

**42. Robinson, J.: *Essays in the Theory of Economic Growth*. London: Macmillan, 1962.

43. Roemer, J.: "Technical Change and the Tendency for the Rate of Profit to Fall", *Journal of Economic Theory*, **16 (1977), 403–424.

*44. Rubin, I. I.: *Essays in Marx's Theory of Value*. Detroit: Red and Black, 1972.

**45. Samuelson, P.: *Foundations of Economic Analysis*. Cambridge, Mass.: Harvard University Press, 1963.

**46. Schoenman, J.-C.: *An Analog of Short-Period Economic Change*. Stockholm: University of Stockholm and Almquist and Wicksell, 1966.

**47. Schoenman, J.-C.: "Interactions of the Marshallian Period as Privileged Base for Positive Theory", unpublished, 1984.

**48. Senchak, A.: "Capital Accumulation and the Duration of the Production, Sales, and Expenditure Processes: the U.S. Non-financial Corporate Business Sector 1963–1977", Ph.D. dissertation, Columbia University, 1982.

*49. Shaikh, A. "An Introduction to the History of Crisis Theories" in *U.S. Capitalism in Crisis*. New York: Union for Radical Political Economy, 1978.

**50. Shaikh, A.: *Marxian Economic Analysis*. Oxford: Blackwell, 1985.
**51. Shaikh, A.: "Profitability and the Current Economic Crisis", *Science and Society*, forthcoming.
**52. Smith, A.: *An Inquiry into the Nature and Causes of The Wealth of Nations*. New York: Modern Library, 1937.
 *53. Sraffa, P.: *Production of Commodities by Means of Commodities*. Cambridge: Cambridge University Press, 1972.
**54. tenRaa, T.: "Dynamic Input-output Analysis with Distributed Activities", unpublished, 1983.
55. van Parijs, P.: "The Falling-Rate-of-Profit Theory of Crisis: A Rational Reconstruction by Way of Obituary", *Review of Radical Political Economics* **12(1) (1980), 1–16.
 *56. von Neumann, J.: "A Model of General Equilibrium", *Review of Economic Studies*, (1945), 1–9.
**57. Weisskopf, T.: "Marxist Perspectives on Cyclical Crisis" in *U.S. Capitalism in Crisis*. New York: Union for Radical Political Economy, 1978.
58. Weisskopf, T.: "Marxian Crisis Theory and the Rate of Profit in the Postwar U.S. Economy", *Cambridge Journal of Economics* **3(4) (1979), 341–378.

INDEX

59

For Product Safety Concerns and Information please contact our
EU representative GPSR@taylorandfrancis.com Taylor & Francis
Verlag GmbH, Kaufingerstraße 24, 80331 München, Germany